CAREERIN(
THE PY

" Galacti dinner .

David White
Xmas '95

CAREERING ABOUT IN THE PYRENEES

by David Whitter

Illustrations by Jean de Lemos

J Buchanan Wilson

Disclaimer
Although this account is based on the true experience of the author,
the names of people and places have been changed and some events
modified to protect privacy, as is customary in works of this kind.

Published by J Buchanan Wilson
PO Box No. 55, Scunthorpe, S. Humberside DN15 8XN

Illustrations by Jean de Lemos

Designed by Alan Gatland

Text Preparation: I T Associates

Printed by Modern Press, Tovil, Maidstone, Kent, England

ISBN 0 9525622 0 0

CONTENTS

CONTENTS

"Clean," - said my *patron*. I casually spread my hands, nails upwards, on the official desk. "Reliable," - I produced a diary and made a little note. "Honest." - I rose from my seat, looked the banker straight in the eye, and offered him my hand to shake. "*C'est bon,*" he said. My first

Preface

customer had accepted me, and I was launched on my new career: window-cleaning in the Pyrenees.

Thirty years of commuting to the Big City; thirty years of paper-pushing in the Big Office; thirty years winning status, a long-service award and a carpet: and suddenly here I was, ladder and leather at the ready, middle-aged and yet on the brink of - Adventure.

True, there had been inklings, over the years: pipe dreams of an away-from-it-all home in the mountains; notions of release from the pettiness of office politics; a desire to take up a personal challenge rather than accept the moving goalposts of Top Management. These were straws in the wind, but nothing more.

Then one day, during a summer holiday in a little sunny town in French Catalonia, I saw him. He was all of six-foot tall, with close-cropped white hair that shone like a beacon. He was leaping up and down a ladder, wash-leather in hand, "like a Jack-rabbit," to use his own expression. "There," said my French friend, "you see a happy man. And yet," he added, in admiration tinged with consolation, "he comes from your country."

It was thus that I was introduced to my *patron*. A few years older than me, he had been at the Normandy landings, which occasioned much respect amongst the local townsfolk. After spending most of his working life in England, he had decided to seek sun and independence in the South of France. Ten years later, bronzed and almost as fit as the commando he had once been, he was thinking of retirement and looking for a successor to take over his little contract cleaning business.

"Why not you, boyo?" he said "The business keeps you solvent; it keeps you busy; and it keeps you *en forme*. You make good

2

amis. What more do you want? Oh yes, *bien sûr*," he added, "there's the *soleil* and the grub. But I've come to take them for granted since leaving Birmingham!"

With early retirement for my wife and myself "on offer," and with the children more or less off our hands, we returned to England, "Why not you?" ringing in our ears.

Thus it was we found ourselves buying and renovating a shepherd's cottage 1000m high in a Catalan village in the Pyrenees, and learning how to become accepted in the local town as 'French' artisans. What fun it has been. What fun it continues to be; for the fun, like the learning, never stops. Why not us? Why not you?

CHAPTER ONE

Home is where the Art is

Dolce domum **D-I-Y**

Frsnce is a big country, five times the size of England. That is why the French think big when it comes to *bricolage* or D-I-Y. Not to be outdone, so do the Catalans. Not for them a nudge of delicate *Polyfilla*, a whisper of *Dulux Apple Blossom White*. When decorating is the order of the day, you need giant-sized imagination and a pair of giant-sized hands. To avert disappointment, it is best to start with a ruin, preferably with a roof-beam or two intact to stop the heavy roof tiles falling in on you.

The roof-beams have the diameter of your waistline after *Mardi Gras*, but you soon appreciate the wisdom of the one in contrast to the folly of the other. To begin with, using a whole tree-trunk means less work. Second, you must allow anyway for about two hundred years of wood-worm feeding, after which the inner core of the beam is so hard the woodworm "break their teeth," as the locals explain. Then you discover that the egg-shaped, grey-green roof-slates, glistening with mica, are extremely heavy. This is not to test your muscles, but to ensure the slates stay in place when the fierce north wind, the *Tramontane*, blows. Not for Catalans the clattering of falling slates at the first hint of autumn.

The roof is held up by dry-stone walls, whose chinks are filled with clay. A metre thick at the base, they provide ample barrier against heat and cold, without the need for cavity-wall insulation, under-floor heating, air-conditioning or other 20th century fads. Furthermore, the walls rarely crack, bow or collapse. The occasional huge bulge to be seen is nothing more than a bread oven, so designed to take away the heat from the interior, maybe add a touch of artistic *fantaisie*.

We took the plunge, and bought an old three-storey house, nestling into the rockface in the tiny Catalan village of *Noullogarret*, not very far from the Catalans' magic mountain, the *Canigou*, and about fifteen kilometres from the nearest town, *Riberal.*

Foreboding turned to admiration at the four-square stability of the structure. I entered the gloomy, tomb-like basement, built into the rock like a cave. Electric flex, threadbare and gleaming faintly, festooned the darkness like a spider's web, where once the family sow had farrowed, and chickens pecked about. The attempt to tangle with 20th century technology had been heroic, but hazardous. The insulation powdered as you watched, like the winding-cloths of some Egyptian mummy. The villagers were mystified at my concern. The lights worked when kicked, so why worry?

Breeches and *bricolage.*

I decided I needed technical assistance. "*Albert's* your man," said my neighbours. "Besides being an electrician, he's an explorer and an expert on caves." True to form, the first thing *Albert* did was to eye the mountain opposite, and delve into a grotto. But not before he had cast off his natty velours trousers and borrowed my working jeans. "Tough," he said, I think referring to the jeans, but he offered no further clarification.

Wise after the event, here let me offer a word of warning. Never lend your trousers to anyone; much less a cave-happy Catalan whose obsession is speleology, house-wiring a mere hobby. If you would remonstrate, consider well. You cannot present a full-frontal *exposé* of your grievances to the Town Hall. Indeed, you are hard put to it to seek consolation, in such *déshabille*, from your nearest neighbour, where kissing on both cheeks is expected.

Later, replete with caving, *Albert* installed himself for months, enjoying my wife's *haute cuisine* for breakfast (English style: even kippers), lunch and afternoon tea (English style: always with buttered scones). Little by little our basement took on the appearance of a nuclear submarine, cables and quivering high-tension dials everywhere. The installation of a circuit-breaker was the talk of the village. Its paintwork was admired, its purpose remained a puzzle. The first time he connected to the mains, the streetlights flickered, as though to prove he had done a thorough job. No doubt he had, but I would like my trousers back .

We next had a carpenter, a Max Wall look-alike, who would have done better to return to the stage. He was the first worker in wood who did not believe in verticals or horizontals. Not hot on screws either. He liked lots of nails and adopted a *laissez tomber* approach to structures. He built me a cupboard with sliding doors to protect my music centre from any approach whatsoever. The doors were so constructed you could not get at the knobs.

A builder was commissioned to repair the balcony and wall. After several months' wait, he was surprised to find we still wanted it doing, and sent his mate. He made quite a good job of it, but forgot to lay the balcony tiles.

Plumbing was a more serious challenge. We had inherited a loo, the pride and joy of the local who had installed it. If so inclined, you could rock yourself to sleep on it. For the less soporific, it had the effect of keeping you very wide awake. One sunny breakfast-time, this neighbour patiently demonstrated, in our living-room, how to lower yourself philosophically, and rise with satisfaction from an imaginary solid-state seat. Caution in descent, patience in ascent were the watchwords. His feet were huge and flat, and planted far apart. Years of practice, perched over holes in the ground, had ensured mastery of the art. He exhibited perfect poise.

The long and short of it

The next problem was the living-room, built into the rockface. What should I do? My English drill could not pierce solid stone. A helpful German neighbour, who possessed the sort of tools which in England you would only find on a Wimpey building site, lent me his grosse *Bohrmaschine*. A cement mixer, a thoughtful birthday present from his girlfriend, rumbled in his kitchen. His vacation was to be a busy one. My nerve failed, however, and I turned once more to locals for advice. "It's a matter of size," they said enigmatically. And so it turned out. We had assorted Catalan dwarfs on Mondays, Wednesdays and Fridays, and Dutch giants on Thursdays and Saturdays The dwarfs put in hall flooring, iron window-bars and a kitchen, (nothing much over knee height,) while the giants installed ventilators and light fittings and generally lofty items. One giant looked in despair at my drawing for the new chimney-piece. He waved his huge hands in the air and said "No! No!, It go p*louf plouf*. To make good home is an art." I gave in. The huge hands swung great hammers. Cement buckets swayed through the window. Eventually a log fire blazed cheerfully. There never was a drawing; but the chimney never goes *plouf plouf*.

Determined not to be intimidated further, I decided the interior decorating would be tackled by me alone. Huge tubs of *crépi*, a stiff porridge-like substance, arrived, without handles and without instructions. Paint brush and roller served for a while, then succumbed to clogging. A lavatory brush was made of sterner stuff, but finally wilted. Eventually I took to hurling the stuff on to the wall by hand, on the principal that some was sure to stick. It did. To my hand. At last I found the Catalans had invented a fiendish machine, much like a mini-muckspreader, for application. It was first-rate on velocity, second-rate on direction, but somehow the job got done. At least the walls were strong enough to take it.

It was high time to flounder in our one luxury: what our imaginative Parisian neighbour calls our *baignoire tumultueuse*. This is a bubble-bath surreptitiously imported from Spain, by lorry load, in a convoy of forty. Surreptitiously? Well, yes. Although we are in the Common Market, where prices are supposed to be harmonised, one had at that time to go through the motions of smuggling to keep the Customs men gainfully employed. But this was Catalonia, on both sides of the border, where everything was larger than life. One lorry was not worth winking at. Forty winks' worth, especially during siesta time, was more like it.

Why were the baths such a good bargain in comparison with their French counterparts, you may well ask, as I did? It is true they were rated 'heavy industrial grade, suitable for continuous use,' but while that assuaged any doubts I may have entertained as to their robustness, it still left me puzzled as to the implications thereof. Further enquiry drew forth a straight-faced, matter-of-fact explanation: They were baths specially reinforced for supply to the round-the-clock massage parlours of Barcelona. No more questions, but the bubbles come in three grades of tumult, and are magnificently stimulating or relaxing, according to personal inclination. Which is, I suppose, just as it should be, even in Barcelona.

CHAPTER TWO

The answer lies in the toil

11

Gardeners' question-time

It was time to pay attention, like a true Brit., to the great outdoors. I determined to build a barbecue. It rose, a noble pile, hand-built from local stone. It remains for me a thing of great beauty, though neighbours say cautiously it is *très rustique* which, being interpreted, means: likely to fall down at any moment. We held an opening ceremony, a match was lit therein, but only two stones cracked and fell in the intense heat generated. It was, in brief, a technological triumph. I now offer prehistoric *rustique* cuisine prepared with micro-wave swiftness: soups heated by the additional internal thermal source of hot stones falling therein during cooking.

What next, I pondered? A shelter, a shady bower, a vine, to protect my guests from the summer sun. Now in an English village the Oldest Inhabitant is always the Expert, and, for that reason, a person to be studiously avoided. In a Catalan village, everyone is an Expert, and impossible to avoid.

Thus it was that I accepted the offer of help with my vine from a multi-talented linguist, water-diviner, Percy Thrower of the region, and - need I say more - professional Oldest Inhabitant to boot.

It began with rabbit droppings. Not mere bucketsful, you understand, but dung by the barrow-load, to be wheeled brazenly down the village street and off-loaded by the megaton onto my modest terrace. The villagers bade me a cautious *Bonjour* as I passed by. Fortunately I did not have to shake hands too often on the way, as the Catalans are very practical. In any case, as the sun and my temperature rose, I could hardly see or hear them for the flies. Such was the ultimate *embarras de richesse*, the vine looked rather vulnerable. I thought dilution might help and approached with a watering can. It was snatched roughly from my hand. The linguist spoke. *"Non! Comprenez?* **No!***"* *"Oui,"* I said hastily, adding to the confusion. I bent down apologetically to remove a flat stone which seemed to have fallen against the vine stem. *"Non!* **No**!*"* said the old man, indicating forceably my lack of expertise. He carefully replaced the stone like a little tombstone in front of the vine. I tried to look both obliging and pious. *"Allez*!*"* he said, and walked away.

Next I erected a little pergola, curiously called a *tonnelle.* I could not imagine what British Rail, or even the SNCF, had to do with my bucolic hide-away. The French tell me theirs is a wonderfully precise language, with a word for everything. I believe them. They often have a single word which has to do for everything. The vine looked promising, as I tied up the tendrils. After all, I was only intending to produce a shady bower, not indulge in viticulture. The whole village turned out to discuss the project. The air was full of circular arguments and round oaths. Next morning when I arose, the vine had been cut down to a foot above the ground.

I examined my conscience. How had I offended? Should I have lowered the barrow and insisted on shaking hands, even proffering a nifty kiss? Should I have stood a little longer in silent prayer by the little tombstone? I sought the advice of the Expert. Perhaps he would forgive me. He clawed the air with his right hand. *"Comprenez*?*"* he said. *"Oui,"* I replied, doubtfully. He shook his head ferociously, and slapped his clawing hand with the other, as if it were a wild thing out of control. *"Non!* **No**!*"* he said. He bent down and began the alarming clawing motion again, this time at ground level. *"Comprenez*?*"* he said. *"Oui,"* I replied, lying in my mounting hysteria. *"Bon,"* he said:*"* Shoots **bad**, roots **good**," and walked away again.

A year later - patience is a virtue - my *tonnelle* was once more a leafy bower, this time with hanging bunches of grapes, like the holiday posters. The Expert suddenly appeared again, unbidden. "Come, *avec* 'ammer!" Did he expect me to lend him a hand, after his toil of yesteryear, I wondered, trotting dutifully after him, hammer at the ready? He led me to the village square, where a game of *pétanque*, or bowls, was in progress. Pointing to a huge metal plate in the centre of the square, he said "Knock!" I knocked. "Pull!" I pulled. A concrete well was exposed, walled with metal sluice gates with handles. "*Encore*, pull!" he said. I pulled, and a foaming wall of water rushed into the void and swept off down an adjacent tunnel. Two wayward *boules* plopped into the torrent. "Jump!" said my mentor. I jumped in and just managed to save the *boules* from being swept away. But the game was, so-to-speak, a wash-out, notwithstanding. I clambered out, replaced the plate, gave a fierce-looking Catalan his *boules* back, shrugged an abject apology, and slunk off, amid threats to my physical wellbeing should I venture to return.

Subterranean Catalonia rumbled as we made our way down to the terrace. There was a noise of many waters. Beneath us no terrace, but a paddy field. An old pipe jutting out of the wall was throbbing like a turbine, and jetting water across the terrace like a manic fire-hose. "*Bon!*" said my Expert, appreciatively. "Water for vine is **good**. Now go to square to **stop it**!"

Horticultural rites

Several weeks later, not at ease with such an anti-social means of acquiring water for my plot, I decided to research alternative technology, which I hoped would be environmentally friendly, as it were. It was thus that I encountered primitive Earth-Mother rites, or so they seemed. An old gardener led me out of the village, to show me how to operate a different watering channel, fed by the river, which would lead directly to my vegetable plot, beside the terrace. I already had a commendable crop of potatoes, which I attributed to my Irish blood. "Not so!" said my horticultural guide. "It's because you set them on a waning moon." This planting rite applies to all root crops - and lettuces, I was informed. In contrast, I learned you plant

14

peas and beans and other leafy produce on a waxing moon, for best results in that department. "But why treat lettuces like carrots, in that case?" I asked, struggling to come to grips with lunar logic. He turned his eyes appealingly skyward, perhaps hoping to get a glimpse of that capricious heavenly body itself, then patiently explained: "Lettuces are planted on the adverse waning moon, because you don't want them to grow too fast and run to seed. *Voilà!*" (Ask a silly question...)

Then he led me upstream, somewhat precipitously, to a little tributary. There, instead of a metal sluice gate to divert the flow, he revealed to me, with modest devotion and no unseemly haste, a soggy repository of antique bras. It turned out they had belonged formerly to *Noullogarret's* most revered female inhabitant, elderly dispenser of herbal remedies, folklore and counsel, and brilliant at roasting wildboar. I realised how little I yet knew of Catalan culture, or rather, horticulture, dependent still for fructification on the Feminine Principle. Gently stirring aside straps and buckles , I released the flow, and the stream gushed forth in the direction of my potato patch. I felt I had discovered a more earthy version of Ingres' inspiration for *La Source*. The only mystery remaining, metaphysical I suppose, is why the old lady, rising seventy and so little endowed forward, should ever have owned such abundance of garments so rich in promise.

"Aux Arbres, Citoyens!"

The grape and the potato may well serve to warm the inner man, but as autumn arrived, at 1000m it was time to anticipate outer chills - and the provision of winter fuel.

My attention was drawn to a militarist document, reminiscent of *La Marseillaise*, thrust imperiously through my letterbox. It was entitled *"Aux Arbres, Citoyens!"* and demanded of every right-minded citizen that he endeavour to "Save the forest." I was basking in a warm, self-righteous glow of ignorance, ready at a moment's notice to sign a petition to use only recycled paper, to avoid leaving picnic litter in the woods, or vote against a motorway: something liberal, democratic and undemanding. Little did I realise what would be expected of me as a true Citizen of the *Commune*, as winter approached. I had heard vaguely that villagers were entitled to free firewood. It conjured up cosy visions of roasting chestnuts at the hearth; even being able to pay electricity bills on receipt. True, I could not see how it squared precisely with the clarion-call "*Sauvons la forêt!*" I was soon to learn.

Only the trees selected by the *forestiers*, a shadowy band of hairy, muscular tree-dwellers whom you never see in broad daylight, were allocated for human utilisation. These trees were wholly hidden from view, a thousand metres higher than the village, some six thousand feet above sea level. Furthermore, they grew far above the forest track, and far above extensive groves of other younger trees, which were to be left strictly unmolested.

Such discoveries seemed curious, but I felt confident that the little matter of tree-felling, log-chopping, and delivery to my doorstep, if not my hearthside, would remain, for an alien like me, wholly academic. Not so. The firewood was 'free' for each Citizen of the Commune, to be sure, by ancient 14th century decree, but you had to go up and get it yourself.

First came the initiation ritual of the chain-saw. I was advised to buy one "to suit my temperament." I was deemed not *féroce* enough to merit a large one. Nevertheless, I felt extremely nasty to know, once I had mastered the art of mixing petrol and oil in the right proportions (only amateurs buy ready-mixed fuel, I was told, scornfully), and had the weapon roaring uncontrollably about my person. Next, I had to learn to turn it off without losing my presence of mind and a finger or two. Then came the delicate art of tightening the heated chain, without dropping minuscule fixing nuts on the leafy forest floor. This could be annoying, I was told. I could well imagine.

After weapon training, the route march: right up into the forest, to find my personal trees, all twenty-five of them, two years' supply, each marked with an x. After a further half-hour scramble up a forty-five degree slope covered with old branches, young trees and undergrowth, I found trees marked w and y. I was a little perturbed. Did x exist? Then I remembered I was on a military exercise. Even though the letters had been drawn out of a hat, it was clear my trees had to be the most inaccessible, as I was still a cadet, and in need of experience. I found the trees at last, behind the others, and higher still.

I realised there was an art in making trees fall in the required direction, but I was not prepared for the problem which arises when the selected tree refuses to fall at all, but nestles comfortably against its neighbour, which, being unmarked, is not for felling. My taciturn Catalan instructor showed me. Reaching high above his head, he cut a metre above the base of the suspended tree. The sawn-off piece plummeted to earth, nearly transfixing his foot. The tree itself slithered down more hesitantly, approaching a lethal vertical angle, or so it seemed to me, an absolute beginner in the art of being a lumberjack. He repeated the operation, and the tree took ages making up its mind where to fall, doubtless looking for a human target. Finally it crashed down, and I approached from my vantage point, halfway up an adjacent hillside, to see if my instructor was still alive. "All in a day's work", he said, counting his legs.

After that, I hardly dared ask him how to get the trees down to the track, there being neither river nor elephant to hand. "Cut off the branches and push," he said, being a man of few words. I did just that, sitting on my backside, knees up, with my feet at the ready, then thrusting them sharply out in front of me, so pushing the entire trunk, top first, down the slope. Sometimes it hardly budged. At other times it gathered momentum and shot down the mountain like a torpedo, carrying with it branches, rocks, and, very likely, unwary ramblers who had not heeded our warning shouts. On reaching the track, such was its velocity, it could easily have swept a vehicle right off the road, had not the wily Catalan woodsmen and hunters parked their trucks at a respectful distance from the chute. I was a little concerned at the carefree proximity of the hunters, wanting to confront neither wild boar nor bullet during the ticklish tree-felling operation. "People sometimes get shot, but not seriously," said my laconic mentor. "It helps to sing as you work, though, if your saw is not in action."

I draw a veil over the return to civilisation. The trees were sawn into logs and loaded on the neighbour's lorry. He helped, but there were twelve good-sized beech trees to tackle between us. I returned in the lorry, having knocked the sump off a friend's van I had previously borrowed to go up to the forest in. I had found that the huge stones embedded in the mountain tracks were quite unrelenting. My friend, fortunately, was less so, and accepted my apologies with a grin.

Now I had only to develop axe-happy muscles for splitting and stacking the wood, remembering, of course, that another dozen or so trees would require my attention the following season.

CHAPTER THREE

Maastricht strictures

La carte before the horse

As a citizen of the European Union, no English man or woman resident in France is legally obliged to possess a resident's permit, or *carte de séjour*. But to be without one is rather like a woman going topless: the authorities don't bat an eyelid provided she stays beached. If she decides to drive a car, go shopping, cash a cheque, or engage in business of any kind, that's quite a different matter: she'll need to be covered. Bra-tops, however, as I had already found out, were easier to come by than *cartes de séjour*.

Before arriving to live permanently in France, we had asked the French Consulate in London what documentation would be required, either mandatory or merely advisable. They counselled my obtaining a *Visa d'Etablissement*, which they assured us would serve the dual purpose of guaranteeing our permanent residence, whether employed or no. After considerable effort on our part, including going to London again for a French medical - superficial, expensive, but very amicable - the *Visa* was issued.

On our arrival in France, no-one, not even the mayor, seemed to have heard of such a document, by now boldly bristling in my passport. We had to begin anew with a fresh set of documentation, this time to acquire the 'non-essential' *cartes de séjour*. Without these, it would seem, we could do practically nothing, except for, metaphorically speaking, lazing topless on the beach. No harm in that option, of course, for either sex, but we were looking for a rather livelier lifestyle. The French Consulate in London refused to part with the original papers, and photocopies were strictly inadmissible. Rather late we discovered that it is by such arcane administrative rituals that middle-class employment in France is maintained at a socially acceptable level.

The village mayor of the day, himself a former immigrant from Spain, relished the challenge. "Ah yes," he pondered, "let's see; you were born in England, while your wife, though *britannique* was born in Japan, *n'est-ce pas?*" "Quite so," I replied, non-plussed. He shuffled through his papers, then, looking me straight in the eye, shot out the question: "Tell me, *Monsieur*, do you remember signing the Treaty of Rome?" The remark was so sudden and surreal I found myself replying in like manner. "Well, yes. In fact, I remember it well, because I had to borrow a pen." Not in the least perturbed, the mayor continued: "I thought so. In that case you, *Monsieur*, have no payment to make for your *carte de séjour*. You, *Madame*, have had the misfortune to be born in Japan. *Donc*, you cannot possibly have signed the Treaty of Rome. *Donc*, for your *carte*, I much regret, you will have to pay a small fee."

More problems lay ahead. Because I had promised to purchase the business by a certain date, I was running short of time. But shortage of time, like absence of paperwork, is an altogether alien concept for the administrators, the *fonctionnaires*. To them delay is as much a perk as a right to a pension. Things were complicated by the fact that the old mayor was replaced by a new one during the bureaucratic hiatus, and the new incumbent was relatively inexperienced. As he was a cowherd, his office hours could also be erratic. At advertised times of opening, he was often not in the *Mairie* or Town Hall, because he was looking for his bull, lost somewhere on the mountain. It was no good turning to the deputy mayor, either, because he had similar problems with goats.

When the new mayor did finally contact both the local *Sous-préfecture* and the more remote *Préfecture*, everyone denied ever having heard of us and said no *dossier* was in existence. The stalemate continued. Then we happened to mention our problem to an American friend who knew 'an important personage' in a position of authority. The American was a descendant of Sir Francis Drake, so I was confident of a successful outcome, barring Spanish Euroveto, as the French respect *pétanque* players. And so it turned out. The *dossier* was located on a window-sill where it had been peacefully gathering dust. "A little local difficulty," they said.

Alas, my joy was short-lived. True, my *carte* arrived, but I found it to be a temporary one, good for one year only. This would not allow me to register at the Chamber of Trade to take the training course essential, in turn, for me to start work as planned. By the November, some twelve months since the problems began, the *carte* was still awaited. It transpired the 'local' difficulty had become national. Paris was involved. For all I could discover, it could as well have been Brussels or the United Nations. Again instant rectification was promised. "It's in the post," was the threadbare word of cheer. But it wasn't. Hotlines hummed between Heads of State (for all I know) and our lowly village cowman before it finally arrived.

Horse-sense had prevailed at last.

That year was the anniversary of the French Revolution, and talk was of the guillotine. It was not hard for me to think of suitable candidates.

Stage fright

Becoming an artisan or craftsman in France requires that you be artful and crafty at the same time. The reason is because it is in the interests of the bureaucrats to make life as skillfully complicated as possible so that they themselves become indispensible.

Should you want to clean windows, for example - a simple and humble trade, one would have thought, - you need not only to acquire wash-leather, bucket and water, and maybe a ladder, but full artisanal registration. After the acquisition of a *carte de séjour*, itself no doddle, as we have seen, you must perforce go 'on the stage.' No, this does not mean treading the boards, but undertaking a training course on running a business, something equally daunting. Indeed, I found it required a true grasp of the drama.

Every would-be seeker after *artisanal* limelight must turn up at the regional Chamber of Trade for two weeks of lectures, memory work and rehearsal before being awarded the equivalent of his or her Equity card. Our course was postponed, as it happened, by another which was entitled, to all intents and purposes, "How to fool your taxman." I felt this was a good omen, and my appetite sharpened.

A motley gathering we were, to be sure, as we faced our director, - it seemed he was none other than Omar Sharif himself, - on that first apprehensive morning. There was a half-baked couple intending to be the world's first theatrical bakers. He was clad in the latest sharp fashion: bold cut to trouser and jacket and frilly shirt; but still he contrived to look like the lead in Mother Goose. She wore tight-fitting white pantalons, veined in dire mauve, topped by a swash-buckling bright yellow leather coat, licenced to kill, - or at least intimidate - with *savoir-faire*. Yet her expression was that of Wol in the A.A.Milne classic, where wisdom succumbed to overall torpor, at least during daylight hours.

There was a diminutive, pretty girl with a shy smile, scarcely out of knee-stockings, who turned out to have already gone bankrupt twice. Her husband was as head-over-heels in love with her as she was once more head-over-heels in debt. She clearly believed that the world of cut-throat competition was a Wonderland over which she could have little control, but through which she could wander aimlessly but aimiably until success came her way. A perfect Alice, her self-confidence was unassailable.

A double-act provided drama reminiscent of Greek Tragedy. They were to be roofing experts. She, the brains of the enterprise, prayed ever to Zeus, God of rain, so that the *clientèle* might appreciate the shortcomings of their existing structures. He, the brawn, worshipped Phoebus Apollo, that work might proceed unhindered by inclement weather. Their rapport was thus fatally flawed from the start.

An ex-Master Butcher, older than the rest of the cast, was brooding because he was obviously 'resting.' He wished to take up the chopper again. He was dark, quiet, and ruthlessly clear-cut in calculations. Clearly the block would soon again be his.

There was a blustery, garrulous, red-faced comedian, always first with commentary, who knew the punch-line to every story, and could doubtless have upstaged the Ancient Mariner. There was a beautiful leading lady, without a trace of muscle, aspiring none-the-less to master-masonry; a leading man with a golden voice who was cut out to top the bill at window-dressing and fascia renovation; a *chou-chou* seller, who sported a debonaire cravat like David Niven; and a genuine *faux-naif* candle maker. Lastly there were several hopefuls destined to be spear-carriers all their lives; and ourselves, aspiring only to walk-on parts, having some difficulty with the spoken word.

Each of us, in our inimitable way, caused mayhem. Every time Omar said "No-one ever has a negative turn-over," the little *chou-chou* seller from the beach said plaintively: "But I do! Even with my allowance from *Maman*, when nobody buys any *chou-chou* and my stock goes stale!" The artistic candle-maker hoped to evade all tax under the pretext of being an *artiste libre*. She also argued she need not pay insurance for an employee. "Whyever not?" said Omar, exasperated. "Any employer who pays an employee wages has also to pay his or her insurance, *artiste* or no." Not at all crushed, she responded: "Well, you see, he stole money from the till, and is now making up for it in weekly installments. In fact, he is paying me, so perhaps he should be paying **my** insurance, *n'est-ce pas?*"

But I forget. Last, but not least, there was the Clown. With the clown's astonished face, and nothing operative behind the bouncing eyebrows, this fall-about comic explained cheerfully that he sought no trade, being happy to float above all the dialogue and stage directions "like a glider." "*Je suis planeur,*" he gaily admitted. Yet, whenever debate was at its most intensive, or explanation at its most critical, Clown would say something so irrelevant that we all had to take a five-minute break to recover. In his way, he was quite useful.

So much for the *dramatis personae*. As for the plot of the drama, being devised by *fonctionnaires*, it seemed at first fiendishly complex and pointed to fiendish conclusions for the unwary. But somehow or other we persevered. We learnt about simple accountancy practice and employment legislation, sick pay and pension benefits. We worked at balance sheets, tax returns and VAT. Later, we were grouped in syndicates to launch 'mock' enterprises, and justify our profitability forecasts. Whenever we were at a loss, through inexperience or language difficulties, we always found there were others similarly at sea. The director was patience personified. In all, we found the mandatory course extremely useful, and well worth the small fee. The true cost is subsidised by the Chamber of Commerce.

We were as pleased as Punch when, after about six sessions spread over two weeks, we won our certificates and it was our turn to take a bow.

La Donna e mobile

The time had come to equip myself with a suitable vehicle for my work. I set off to the Big City, *Perpignan,* for a test drive.

Now the Catalans pride themselves on being twice as good as the English, at least. For example, where we have two rush-hours, they have four. Of these the second, the rush to midday lunch, is the most resolute. The dealer explained. Every full-blooded husband has to rush home at midday, not only for the huge obligatory meal, but to see whether or not any new babies ressembling the postman have arrived. (British milkmen, there's food for thought). By any measure, an exhilarating time for a test drive.

The first car I tried, a *Peugeot,* affronted at having a stranger - and a *perfide Albion* at that - at the wheel, decided enough was enough. It could drive **me**. I was obliged to stay in the gear it chose, until it felt like a change. This normally happened when approaching parking bollards, which modestly duck out of sight as you get near. They are made of cast iron or re-inforced concrete, and are the pride and joy of Catalan mayors and local panel-beaters. At any speed over 30kph the car roared in manic delight, like an omnibus liberated from its OAP passengers after a day's outing to the sea.

The second car, a sleek and sophisticated *Lancia*, exhibited an unnerving grating noise as I swerved erratically round corners, as though grinding its teeth in Latin resentment.

At last I found her, a *Fiat Panda*, flirtatious and a *Lady* at every flounce of the accelerator. Time for the open road.

The salesman allocated for the drive, it was explained, would be polite and attentive at all times. He had been specially chosen to deal with foreigners' failure to comprehend French, or French high-tech, or both. If in doubt, the two commands to obey, in contending with the midday Formula One trials were "brake" and "accelerate," preferably the latter. I recalled a friend's account of how she had failed her French driving test for not overtaking and cutting in before oncoming traffic arrived "while there was just enough time to do it."

I was, I admit, a slow learner. Not so the *Fiat*. Her deportment was fiery and feminine. On the autoroute she took command like a *Diva* at *La Scala*. The horrendous oaths of the starving commuting cuckolds blasted my eardrums. But to her the chorus of klaxons, the *bravissimo* of brakes were music. I braked. I accelerated. I even swore loudly - once. The salesman swore frequently, but s*otto voce*. My new *inamorata* just shrugged and hit a high note. She flirted disgracefully with both of us. She waltzed me daringly behind a roundabout boasting a melodramatic palm tree and I was smitten. "**Stop!**" said the salesman, - I think in English - and got out. The overture was over: our duet was about to begin.

Little did I realise how soon this marriage of two minds would be put to the test.

Priorité adroite

In the France of the old franc one became accustomed, when motoring through sleepy sun-kissed villages, to giving way to anything materialising from the right, be it donkey-cart, wobbly teenager on shrieking *mobylette*, or an old widow with a bundle of firewood to her back.

Nowadays, with European 'harmonisation,' the old rule no longer applies, strictly speaking. But beware: this has merely resulted in an even more imaginative interpretation of the essential elements of road safety. The test is now not just of right-handed dexterity, as it were, but of all-round agility: spatial, mental, and psychological.

I know, because all three, as it happens, are categories encountered on any 'normal' day downtown in *Riberal*.

There is one old fellow who distracts you from looking at the direction his feet are pointing in by bidding you a cheery *Bonjour*! apparently before walking smartly out of your path. Not so. His feet, by prior mutual arrangement, are pointing towards their customary resting place, the *Café Chez Pierrot,* and that's where he is headed, - although even he doesn't know it - right athwart your front bumper *en route.*

Another disturbs by looking quite dead. He is grey of face and usually stationary. Of a sudden, however, you discover he has feet which are mobile. Moreover, they have characters totally independent from each other. The left foot shuffles hesitantly and apologetically in the gutter, so that you think their owner is politely awaiting your passage; but then the right foot lunges suddenly in the air, poised alarmingly at the horizontal, as though to stave in your nearside door if *priorité* is denied.

Neither Catalan, it would seem, is aware of any shortcomings in the directional control of his limbs. It pays, therefore, to be alert to imminent change in direction and velocity of each owner's every extremity - before he is.

27

The mental tests are a little more exacting. There is a merry fellow, whose hilarity hides sudden lurches of frame and temperament. He often bursts out laughing, as though at some private joke, just before launching his massive form directly at your front wheels. Even after the squeal of brakes, he continues to giggle, ruminatively, at the astonishing revelation that he is still in one piece.

On a narrow mountain road, some nine foot across, an ancient gnome-like figure in glasses approaches riding a *mobylette*, a six-foot wide agricultural implement strapped at right-angles to his back. You stop. But he wobbles forward and past, scraping your door with the aforesaid rural tool. The test, you realise, is not one of physical, but verbal, reaction. Shortcomings in French vocabulary may, in such a crisis, be an asset. I intended to cry out: "Get **bigger** glasses!" In the event, that would have been deemed a total failure as a response, lacking that vital Catalan element of aggresive imagination. By good fortune, what I actually said, with wondrous innacurate precision, was: " *Obtenez les lunettes plus larges!*," which meant, to be exact, "Get **wider** glasses!" In effect, *le mot juste*. I felt I was progressing.

Again, on a winding narrow mountain road you find there is a driver behind you, furiously tooting. You pull in to the edge of the precipice, gingerly, but crossly, annoyed by Catalan impatience. Your rival draws alongside, stops, and politely winds down his window. You wonder if the rear end of your cherished vehicle has come adrift and gone hurtling down the mountainside. But the other driver merely asks you the time! Yes, it is nearly *midi*, when all things Catalan must stop. "Time for *le pic-nic*," he says "*Bon appétit!*"

For the truly *recherche* example of the psychological test, Authority must be involved. The acid test of sanity (and suitability to hold a driving licence) has doubtless been instigated by the French Driving Test Authorities themselves. It is to find yourself, when approaching road works, waved on by a man waving a **red** flag.

After such experiences, you need a quiet relaxing job. Like window-cleaning.

CHAPTER FOUR

Window on the world

It's not what you do, but how you say it

My apprenticeship in window-cleaning was to be the longest of my life. Trying to fly planes the right way up for the RAF in Canada ("Prairies not flat enough for you, old boy?"); learning inorganic chemistry in order to convince customers my Multi-national employer's plastic packaging was the best ("Never mind if the film won't wrap, concentrate on the quality of the polymer's biaxial orientation"); editing serious speeches for a foreign Chairman in the 80s, whose pride and joy was his mastery of the English idioms of the 40s ("Wizard opportunity, this Common Market, as we are being Europeans, if we can make first Japan's sales go for a Burton, gentlemen chaps"); nothing in my previous career was to measure up to the exactitude of this new experience. Why? Because I found myself in the hands of a perfectionist whose pride in his work was infinite. Panic at the unforeseen professionalism of the trade gradually turned to gratitude, as I mastered the art of bucket and leather, and the wily ways of water on windows.

An even greater problem turned out to be my linguistic short-comings. I never thought my degree in English Language, with smatterings of Anglo-Saxon and Old Norse, long mislaid, would form an essential basis for success in such a modest trade, but I gravely underestimated the linguistic fluidity of my aquatic tutor, and the subsequent giddy angle of the learning curve. Two languages, English and French, I could just about manage, but the unselfconscious flavouring with Welsh and a dash of Catalan made four. On top of that I had to include the unfamiliar technical terms of the trade, cast about me like confetti at a shot-gun wedding. For survival I needed to take on board, willy-nilly, *mouilleur*, (soaker), *raclette*, (wiper) and *gratteur*, (scraper). So that made five. I also reckoned without fact that all tongues were in use simultaneously.

The conversation, or rather monologue, for I was a submissive, if not cowed, student, eager to please, went something like this:

"Put yer *eau* in the *seau* and yer *peau* in the *eau*. *D'accord?*"

"Get yer *mouilleur* and *raclette*, boyo, and don't leave *traces* or *taches*. It's 'ot in the *chaleur*. 'Yer average *nettoyeur comme moi* prefer yer *hiver* even if it *pique* a bit. *Llavors, Dai-bach*, always, look you, pour yer mucky *eau* at the base of an *arbre* and not in the main *carrer*. Them *plantanes* get right *secs* in *été* and need a good *arrose.* "

Six months later came the moment of truth. I was by now trusted to work on my own, unsupervised. I was up a ladder, cleaning the windows of a bank. Two English tourists, *très rosbifs* paused below. Clearly they couldn't understand the security lock. "Damned Frogs. Where's the bloody phrase-book?" Ruffle, ruffle. Then, seeing me: *"Pardonnez moi, pouvez-vous* help *nous* enter bank, *oui?"* "Of course, just press the button," I said. They recoiled in astonishment. "These Frogs can't half talk English well," they muttered, "even bloody window-cleaners! It's this Common Market. Next thing is they'll be over in Blighty taking our fellers' jobs."

I felt I had made it at last.

All human life is there

I know of few occupations where you get to know so many individuals so quickly and so well, while enjoying the benefits of changes of scenery and modest excercise. Postmen or milkmen qualify, perhaps, but there are no milkmen in France and postmen often have to contend with ferocious dogs, (if not enraged commuting husbands). Dogs, truth be told, of the wolf or woofter variety, troubled me from time to time, but I always had the advantage of a bucket of water to hand. The bonus, par excellence, was the weather. Early morning in winter-time could be crisp enough to make your fingers tingle, but the sun was usually sufficiently warm by mid-morning to entice you to cast off the extra pullover or padded *gilet*. Of course it rains from time to time, but the weather usually satisfies itself with an occasional downpour, rather than the unremitting drizzle you get so often in England. The downpours, when they occur, are soaking, since gutters and spouts are rare, and when present, are decorative, rather than functional. The little green gargoyles don't drool: they vomit. To avoid saturation it is time to seek *Chez Pierrot*, and ponder gleefully on the increase in trade the muddy, misdirected torrents are creating. From November on you can sip a winter-warmer. The name on the Alsace label is '*Bière de Christmas*,' but the merrier locals can only get their tongues round the phrase '*Bière de Noël.*' This is still a misnomer, however, since it always stays on tap until Easter. At this point it is deftly replaced by a similarly fortifying '*Bière de Mars.*''

The sun is soon out again, and shutters and smiles open up like flowers. Your customers await. To begin with they seemed merely quaint. Yet how soon, on getting to know them better, I came to disdain my purblind, tourist's eye. And what an advantage I had, plying my trade, to increase my respect for a laid-back philosophy of life so different from my own bustling preoccupations. There was sensitivity in attitudes suited to a climate boisterous but benign; and wisdom in a way of life vociferous on the surface, but tolerant beneath. I hope that, while my jaded eye was open to absurdity, it soon learned to look askance at patronization.

In such a mood of light-hearted enlightenment, I came to realise what an advantage a ladder could be.

A barber of civility

With a shop-sign at eye level I found the perspective validates totally the *cliché* of the fly on the ceiling. Quite innocently you overhear intimate conversations as though you were the Invisible Man. (Here's an invaluable tip for gossip columnists: buy a ladder and get up it! You will find all your copy awaiting you, just two metres below.) One example will suffice; modesty forbids further revelations from my aery confessional.

There is a house, to all appearances unremarkable, except for its garden ornaments. In every corner, nook and cranny you stumble over an *òbjet d'art*. A gnome grins beneath each consciously deposited boulder. An eruption of ornate palms suggests Nature has won through, to provide an oasis in a concrete desert. But no: behind the waving fronds a furtive fountain boasts cement dolphins. Wherever paved pathways intersect, a discarded stone wheelbarrow hints at horticultural petrification. Here and there, but nowhere near water, crouches a diminutive bridge, such as you find infuriating when playing Crazy Golf. Wherever possible, a cherub is poised to surprise you, leaving you unprepared for the *Grotto*. This is intended as a truly irresistable *pièce de résistance*. Within, a mock marble Venus pleads with each passer-by to adjust her immodest drapery.

Perhaps that should have provided a clue. Because the story floating upwards towards the innocent shop-sign from the two nearest nethermost nodding female heads was that the owner of this most '*Homes and Garden*' garden was a wealthy recluse from Parisian high society, where he had moved in the most arty of avant-garde artistic circles. He had become a curiosity much savoured by our plain but sagacious country-folk. There was more to come. His fiercest rival in artistic endeavour was, according to this scandalous chit-chat, a hairdresser in the region. To my innocent eye, he was a very civil practitioner of the art of coiffure, of irreproachable virtue.

"He is commited to being thought the most artistic person in town, you know. He keeps going to Paris to talent-spot at young female hairdressers' competitions," murmured the hat below. So what? I thought. "He returns with urns. And cups. And salvers. He claims they are prizes he's won. His shop is bulging with them." Again, why not? And good for him! "They say he gets them flamboyantly engraved himself, to flaunt his artistry."

I reflected on this curious line of argument. It was true he wore an assortment of outfits which might be considered a mite 'flamboyant': black morning coat, with dress shirt and shiny lapels; green and grey Austrian Tyrolean jacket with golden buttons; a beige toga seemingly acquired from the wardrobe mistress of *I Claudius*. And he's the only person I've ever known who wears spats. But I believed he dressed that way out of sheer personal *joie de vivre*. Nor was he the only hairdresser indulging in exotic attire. His female counterpart, at the other end of the town, frequently sported leopard-skin bandannas, see-through T-shirts and black leather Toreador pants. So try as I might, I could not picture him engaging in a grim, no-holds-barred glamour **competition** with anybody, much less a rich recluse, never to be seen strolling the provincial boulevards of *Riberal*. His modesty and natural flair itself made him far too *sympa* a character - **and** he was good at sports.

But the preposterous musings of the owner of the more frenzedly nodding headgear could not be tamed. She revealed that another female acquaintance of hers had been offered "one of **those arty** photo magazines" to read while awaiting her shampoo, "just because she was Dutch." There was a moment's silence. Then the other hat started to jiggle. "I only get offered *Paris-Match*," it replied. Her overheated imagination said it all. Never before had I observed outrage and wistfulness expressed simultaneously in vibrating feathers. All human life was there.

'*La souplesse dans la rigueur*'

As a cleaner, it pays to cultivate a rare sensitivity. Without being party to the private lives of any of your customers, you are permitted, by hapchance, glimpses of individual behaviour, quirks of personality otherwise revealed only in the relaxed privacy of the marriage-bed or in the conspiratorial intimacy of the psychiatrist's couch. Six feet up a ladder you are below stairs. With your job description consigning you to a modestly lowly estate, you rise effortlessly from rubbing managerial desk-tops to rubbing managerial shoulders: *fraternité*, if not *égalité*, at one meek swipe. Such is the lack of snobbery, and generosity of spirit, of the French. That is, provided you remain tactful and observe *la politesse*.

What, one would think, is more impersonal than the uptight armour of your local bank clerk's desk? Yet take a peep behind. When the faceless pen-pushers have departed, lo! you find each desk is as personalised as your garden shed or kitchen; each waste-paper basket as revealing as your domestic refrigerator or bathroom cabinet. You find that the grim-faced cashier who rarely says *Bonjour* is as self-indulgent as a sultan, and feasts daily on chocolate creams. The pleasant girl who chats cheerfully while cashing your cheque is in terminal emotional turmoil, as revealed daily in the contorted shapes of tens of jettisoned paper-clips. Behind anonymous monitor screens lurk those reassuring cuttings, paper-backs, pipes and knitting patterns which smack of humanity, after all.

Yet how easy it is for apparent authority to dominate. One evening, after the bank had closed, I was cleaning, unobserved, behind the hole-in-the-wall cash dispenser. A car drew up in the road outside, and an English couple got out. While the husband was locking the car, his wife crossed the road and attempted to withdraw cash. "*Algie!*" she cried, "it says '*hors service*,'" (she pronounced it **'horse'** service;) "What does that mean?" Algernon had not heard her call for help, so I could not resist responding through the wall behind the machine, in what I hoped was a suitably computerised helpful Dalek voice: "Out-of-order; repeat: out-of-or-der" "*Algie! Algie!*" cried the woman, "the machine just spoke to me!" "Stupid woman!" Algernon replied, "Always imagining things. And you got no money out, anyway. You really must learn about technical things." "But it **did**, it **did**; - and **in English**!" she said, as they wandered away.

Occasionally, of course, you meet your betters face to face. It is then your obligation to see that things remain decorous - and under control. One evening I arrived to clean the self-same bank. In the boardroom a meeting of all members was still in progress. The topic was the management challenge of implementing '*la souplesse dans la rigueur*'. Clearly this call to the colours had exemplified '*la rigueur*,' for it was after hours. But '*la souplesse*' was also in evidence, as six large bottles of *muscat* sweet white wine had been consumed the while.

When the meeting finally broke up a wet floor confronted the management as they prepared to depart. Cannily I had contrived to leave dry an exit route along a narrow band of red tiles. After their discussions all felt they should politely defer to the principle of *noblesse oblige*. They attempted to 'toe the line,' as it were. However, the *rigueur* implicit in forming a disciplined Indian file of senior executives was more than the *souplesse* of their libations could cope with. I wondered hazily what the French equivalent was to 'British Constitution," and pondered the wisdom of suggesting an equivalent verbal test, in the interests of their safe driving, you understand. As they tiptoed so politely out of the door, I demurred. I felt any interjection on my part, apart from thanking them profusely for their consideration, and wishing them *Bonsoir,* would have smacked too much of *rigueur*, and not enough of s*ouplesse*.

I added the impressions made by their erratic footsteps to my discreet store of individual idiosyncracies. How precious they are in these days of high-tech demarcation. And how honoured my position as caring custodian.

Light fantastic toe-hold

As time passed, my encounters with Catalan DIY *bricolage* in *Riberal* became increasingly unpredictable in *dénouement*, albeit wholly predictable in scale. It was all to do with *la fantaisie*, which implies the Catalans' obsession with the haphazard and the sloping, their casual disrespect for the vertical and horizontal, and their awe-inspiring disregard of stability in all structures save in their own simple homes, where Catalan charity begins. As I surmised from my first-hand domestic experiences of add-on *fantaisie*, (once four-square, four wall foundations are established), it reflects the nostalgia these people, relegated to the plain, still cherish for the crumbling mountain slopes of their childhood homelands. For them, the giddy Pyrenees themselves are a vindication of foot-loose imagination run riot.

In its less harmful manifestations, this preoccupation is evident on all posters. 3Ms has a strangle-hold here of the market for scotch tape, sold by the kilometre for attaching gaudy posters, hand-inscribed in purple and green felt pen ink, to all glass surfaces in the town. They possess a common artistic style which is the embodiment of *la fantaisie*. All lettering starts hugely, bottom left, then rises crookedly to top right, diminishing in size *en route*. The effect on perception of normal perspective is alarming. It's as though you are on your knees, looking side-long and upward in supplication. On a ladder it threatens balance of mind and body simultaneously. You lose your toe-hold on sanity and safety both. When the posters are affixed to moving surfaces, such as sliding doors, calamity is never far away.

Because of my preoccupation with this phenomenon, I allowed the sliding doors of an insurance agency to do away with a brand-new wash-leather, as they slid, to all appearances, uphill, swooping back down squeakily to shed shredded leather and an advertisement for making shrewd provision for an unpredictable future at my feet.

La fantaisie is far worse in three dimensions, as in shop-window design. It is a pre-requisite of the style that all floors shall slope, all angles be acute, and all fixtures belie the very term. It is amazing how mere access to a shop window can cause the collapse not only of fittings, but of fixtures too. In one bijou, miniscule boutique, offering diminutive *woolly pullies*, each a *fantaisie* in itself of bobbly mini-diagonals, my merest admiring touch brought down not only a fantastic curtain, but also a brass rod and plaster rococo fittings. This in turn revealed electric cable, water pipes, a tin shelf with discarded cigarette packet, a folded copy of *L'Indépéndant*, and a scribbled estimate, presumably never presented. The *bricoleur*, or jerry-builder, evidently found the job beyond him, and made a quick getaway. Or perhaps he became immured in one of the more acute angles.

To take another example. I encountered a pharmacy where display packets of herbal remedies for constipation showered down on your humble cleaner from a great height, when he had but prudently clenched his sphincter in bending low to tend his bucket. More strangely, they descended again immediately on being placed back on the shelf. Could the powers that be be imagining that they were dealing with a costive foreigner where repetition was the only way get through, as it were? My wondering and worried examination of the shelf resulted in torn fingerends. The packets were balancing on the points of screws, crookedly inserted, (to further the *fantaisie* theme?), and longer than the shelf was thick.

One of the hazards is to be mistaken for the proprietor, and thus be expected to be *au fait* with things fantastic offered for sale.

I was cleaning a restaurant. It has little to offer in the way of food, but does a roaring trade in Advanced Art. In ridding the window of a huge menu flaunting barbecued rabbit escaping uphill, I found myself unable to dispose discretely of a flamboyant impression - in bright scarlets, blues and yellows - of a trio of what I had to admit were merrily copulating weasels. Maybe they were stoats. But not rabbits, at least. In their case the customary fantastic angle of portraiture fell into place, as it were. Now I am English enough to be conversant with the ways of Mother Nature, but clearly not French enough to cope with blatant troilism, - at least not in a restaurant offering barbecued rabbit at a provocative angle. Unfortunately a potential buyer entered just as I was trying to hide the Opus behind a leaning piano: it was a large canvas, you understand. The buyer showed great interest and I think I could have made a sale, had I not feared he might be from Interpol or the RSPCA (Overseas Branch.) I pleaded total ignorance of Advanced Art - and weasels (or stoats), - and backed diagonally out of the restaurant, keeping the buyer at bay with my bucket.

Caveat emptor

"Touristes! Attention! Danger!" The message dominating the entire window of yet another pharmacy was unmistakable. The vivid scarlet felt pen lettering occupied a scroll as big as a tombstone. Quivering with concern, the Gothic script forecast

the doom of every hapless visitor who might foolishly pay no heed. Huge hand-drawn insects wielding enormous probosces warned that their bite was instantly painful and the effects lasting. More insidiously, bulbous-eyed bugs claimed to pass on debilitating diseases on mere unnoticeable contact with bare unwary human flesh. Against a background of innocent blue crayon depicting the Mediterranean, lurid sea-creatures, all spines and claws, promised excruciating rashes and gashes, while peaceful mountain scenery erupted with vipers and scorpions whose venomous threat was unmistakable.

Once over the pharmacy threshold, however, your holiday could be assured, and your person protected, by the speedy purchase of the specially prepared range of lotions, potions and prophylactic pills on offer - at expenditure (in the circumstances) trivial indeed.

Such advertising, while attention-grabbing, was nothing compared with the salesmanship to be encountered. During a mere half-hour of window-cleaning within the pharmacy itself, I found small and then large irritating lumps emerging at wrist and ankle, my most vulnerable extremities. Close examination of window-sill and display area, before and behind the afore-mentioned scroll, revealed a lively and doubtless replete host of bugs and insects much resembling (if a little smaller) those extravagantly depicted. When further scrutiny of these hidden persuaders revealed a withered reptile, albeit a harmless baby frog, I decided it was time to leave: without payment or purchase. Modern medicaments I can tolerate, and even their promotion, but I draw the line at the witchcraft of your latter-day apothecary.

Token of respect

Pharmacists, alas, cannot remedy all ills, even in Catalonia. Occasionally, it is cold and wet, which, for the aged and infirm, can be depressing. Since retired folk choose to live here for the kind climate, when the temperature does fall and stay low for any length of time, the number of funerals tends to rise sharply.

Because the church is in the town centre, this causes frequent traffic jams and parking problems, as *cortèges* wind their way slowly and sedately through the narrow streets. It may appear unseemly to be concerned about getting on with work at such times, but life must go on, and a way found to continue serving the living while respecting the departed. It is quite a subtle excercise in tactful public relations, having been obliged to park streets away from a waiting customer's window, to cross the town square, meekly and devoutly, mop and bucket in hand, and nudge one's way wetly past mounds of weeping mourners.

Finally, I hit on a symbolic gesture which I trusted might supplant crassness by comfort, in the reddened eyes of the habitually bereaved. Instead of lowering head and accoutrements in dutiful (and painful) respect, I took to raising my little ladder slowly in the air, so that it pointed optimistically to a higher realm, as I passed discretely by. You never know, I thought it might help raise the spirits of those left below. I make no claims of its effectiveness in respect of the departed.

If at first you don't succeed, celebrate, celebrate celebrate again

I have said that the weather is usually benign. So it is, but, like the inhabitants, it can be capricious, especially in Springtime. Either way, such behaviour never fails to inform.

Just to prove the point, it is May 8th and snowing. Such unseasonable weather usually keeps all locals indoors. If they do emerge - for example, under the irresistible national compulsion to buy bread - they will be swathed in woolly jumpers and waterproofs, sporting galoshes and wielding umbrellas.

May 8th, however, is a national holiday, purporting to commemorate Victory in Europe, 1945. Everybody knows this calls for an annual outing, to celebrate. Indeed, to succeed socially, or commercially, or both, in France, one first has to celebrate. Sometimes one even celebrates to prepare for the celebration. And of course one always celebrates after the celebration, if it has been a success. An outing counts as a celebration. It means dressing up in your best bib and tucker, to venture into the town square, and be seen, preferably talking to the mayor, or someone of similar civic worth. If the weather is inclement, no matter. All that happens to activate the plan is that one seeks out *Chez Pierrot* a little sooner than planned, in order to divest oneself as quickly as possible of unbecoming outer storm-wear, and seek social solace under cover.

Apéritif in hand, the next thing is to nudge gently towards the appropriate milieu. The social stratification is eloquent in its understatement. First, given the occasion, are those old enough to have fought in the aforesaid war. It matters little whether they actually did any fighting, or, indeed, given the curious politics of the time, whose side they were on. Given the chance to elaborate, most, for the sake of the ultimate in social acceptability, will swear they were at the *Débarquement*, - the Normandy landings on D-Day. If this were so, on the basis of a spot local head-count, there would not have been much room left on the beaches for the British, Americans or Canadians.

The next group consists of anybody who is somebody: bank managers, lawyers, insurance agents, chiefs of police, the sub-tycoons of the Chamber of Commerce, and all bureaucrats holding sway locally. In fact this group consists of all those you are bound to need, sooner or later, in order to function effectively by day, and sleep easy by night. It is as well to know that, because none of these worthies keeps regular office hours. You are likely only to be able to meet them on celebratory occasions. And only this way can you ever get anything done. This is why there are so many *fête*-days and festivals. Without them France would grind to a standstill.

It follows that the largest group present is indeed made up of people needing things done: shop-keepers, market-stall owners, cafe proprietors, self-employed builders, decorators, retired pensioners, single parents and youths on the dole. Everyone is there, with their wives, adding *son et lumière*, and everyone is made welcome.

Thus social cohesion is born anew of diverse dire necessities; and the self-congratulating midwife is: the celebration.

Since winter in the mountains can be hard, and the taxman harder, it is appropriate that May boasts the maximum opportunities for such jollifications. There is 1st May, Labour Day, when everybody gives everybody else bunches of lily-of-the-valley in commememoration of striking trades unionists in the 19th century who were shot by the police of the time for not going back to work. On 1st May nowadays nobody goes to work, not even the police. But everybody attends one or two celebrations.

There follows Ascension Day, and Pentecost shortly after, not to forget the aforementioned Victory in Europe Day, tucked neatly in between. All are festivals, and have their festive gatherings, where every little local difficulty is ironed out over an *apéritif* or three, so that the townsfolk are ready to greet the summer visitors from Amsterdam to Ashby - de - la - Zouche with smug and smiling unanimity.

But, you may ask, given a world scene of growing hassle and harrassment which, one may suppose, touches even this little community, what if there is an insufficiency of such days, even so? What price the township's effectiveness then?

You need not despair. Have faith in the inimitable wisdom of the local citizenry. If there are too few festive days in the month to guarantee success, someone opens a shop.

From what I have just related, you will no longer be surprised to learn that the new shop may not have anything as yet on show in its windows, except perhaps the pet cat. The premises may not even have its windows clean, even after months of closure. I have personal experience of being called in to give a shop window a quick once-over **after** the tablecloths and huge vases of flowers had all been laid out for the official opening.

Napkins, plates of *petits-fours*, mouth-watering Catalan pastries called *fougasses*, open bottles of *muscat, pastis*, whisky and *Banyuls* all lay within lethal range of my desperately whirling wash-leather.

I need not have worried about the flowers, come to think of it, for in these parts flowers are not only delivered but put proudly on show still bedecked in gaudy ribbons and protective wrappers, overprinted in stripes of glittering gold. For fear their hospitality should pass unremarked, local shopkeepers believe, literally, in gilding the lily.

At five-thirty the celebration begins. The new owners, husband and wife, stop squabbling over her choice of bright yellow paint for the *décor*, and change into their Sunday best, so that they can be picked out. The guests are expected to come as they are, straight from work or siesta. Some prefer, however, to consider the occasion merits 'outing' status, and overdress accordingly.

The first to arrive are the police, who hurry to mount personal guard over the refreshments. Next is the competition. They surreptitiously eye the stock in the window and then, relieved at its paucity, stroke the cat and greet their hosts vociferously, saying what a fine town this is for their kind of trade, provided one has customers who are established. They have, however, known other traders, now out of business, who were, sad to say, over-ambitious.

Insurance agents and firemen are next on the scene. They always arrive as a team on such occasions. They put their heads together and shake them solemnly over an exposed electrical power point and look intently at a hole in the ceiling in which a live cable lolls, awaiting its fitment.

Then comes the big moment. The mayor, tame photographer clicking neurotically at his elbow, parades through the assembly, accompanied by his favourite bank manager, and a posse of *fonctionnaires* from the Chamber of Commerce. The host gives an appropriately flowery speech of welcome, remembering to thank the mayor profusely - exactly what for one is not quite certain - and the crowd sways towards the refreshment tables.

By common consent, the guests tactfully allow the firemen, assuming a quasi-official role, to move the police to one side. Everyone relaxes as the drink diminishes and the decibels increase. A lawyer, eyeing some import/export documentation protruding from under a tablecloth, calls an acquaintance from the tax department over, and they go into a tactful huddle over their whiskys.

The ex-owner, now retired, beams over his *Banyuls* at some old customers of his. Quietly, and then with increasing fervour as he warms to his reminiscences, he explains how things used to be in his, his father's, and his father's father's day. He did not think yellow paint quite right, and one should never be able to see the stairs leading to the stockroom. It was unseemly, and might well attract thieves. The insurance agent nods in agreement, and makes a little note.

At last, all bottles empty, all curiosity assuaged, and all commercial and social missions accomplished, people begin to drift away. "Are you opening for business tomorrow?" queries a departing guest. "Oh no," replies our host," tomorrow is Ascension Day, remember: a day for public celebration."

CHAPTER FIVE

The generation game

What's in a name?

D uring my first year as *nettoyeur* many had failed to realise I was not my *patron's* son. This son had previously shown some interest in replacing his father on the latter's retirement, but meanwhile had branched out successfully into a painting and decorating business. By the time retirement loomed, and I had appeared on the scene, he preferred to continue his newly established enterprise, and allow me to step into his father's shoes. There was thus some confusion in the minds of several customers, who jumped to the conclusion that, because I was clearly British, I must also be my *patron's* son.

This mistake in generation was embarrassing. Let me explain why. I hope I have already made it clear that my *patron*, with his shining, silver crew-cut, was an exceptional fellow. I held him in great awe as a perfectionist, and as someone who had really and truly participated in the Normandy landings as a youth. He was a chap clearly used to going hard at it and never taking no for an answer. Even so, had the rumour of our relationship been true, the fact that he was a mere eight years older than I would have made such youthful prowess at parenthood indecent, even in French eyes.

It was high time to persevere, and try to lose my ill-defined status. I decided to attack head-on my customers' failure to grasp my name. *Monsieur Incognito* would not do any longer. Progress at establishing the pronunciation of *Whitter* was slow and painful. I was called, tentatively, "*Weetakaire,*", then, with growing confidence based on schoolroom English, "*Weentaire.*" This was a problem, as there were, for all I knew, British *Winters* already in the region, and I did not want cheques for my hard-earned toil paid into the wrong account.

I finally hit on a ruse. "I begin work at '*huit heures*' in the morning;" I explained; "Remember that, and you'll get my name right, more or less." So *Monsieur 'Huit heures'* I became, and my *patron's* juvenile precocity was relegated to anecdote among those elderly customers for whom eight o'clock in the morning was not a time of day with which they were familiar.

I felt pleased to be established with a name as well as a reputation, and at ease with the world.

But woe betide the complacent. On the Monday I was laid back. On Tuesday laid low. On Wednesday laid up - in hospital.

Mushrooms and malady

The label on the medicine bottle read: '***VOIE ORALE***'. As dusk gently enfolded me in my hospital bed, the huge day-glo upper-case letters pulsated, like a neon sign, just out of reach on my bedside locker. My eyeballs ached, and my mind tossed and turned, restless with curiosity. I was used to the British tea-spoon-wagging warning: 'It is dangerous to exceed the stated dose,' and the obligatory mumbo-jumbo of the age-old ritualistic adage: 'Shake the bottle,' executed in elegant copperplate lettering. But why '***BY MOUTH ONLY***,' in strident technicolor? 'How else?' I thought, sleepily. I was soon to learn.

Indeed, the learning curve in a French *clinique* is both steep and astonishing.

Anticipating the brusque, barrack-square precision of the NHS, I was instantly disarmed by the politeness of the procession of figures which flitted past the foot of my bed on my first day. There was the surprising ubiquitous acknowledgement that there really was someone in the bed, and that someone was me, with a name (albeit the equivalent of 8am) as well as a malady. I was also taken aback by the number of professionals, each of whom knocked at my door before entering, and asked if I minded being disturbed. Surgeon and cleaning-woman alike, each treated me as though I were a Royal Personage holding a private audience with favoured supplicants at my own bidding.

Yet in the eyes of the State I was a mere 'French' artisan, with minimum paid-up obligatory health insurance.

Not only were my visitors numerous, but an astonishing range of professions was represented. One thing they all had in common; they each thought of themselves as offering me a service; proudly, it is true, but a service nonetheless, which I could accept or decline. If in response to their approach, I engaged them in even a short conversation, they reacted with delight to be upgraded thereby from servant to guest.

An initial topic of conversation, common to all, was food. When they learned I lived in the mountains, their eyes glistened, and the subject was instantly narrowed to mushrooms. Every Frenchman is obsessed, not with wine, as one may suppose, but with mushrooms. This gushing gastronomic exchange, which soon became predictable, was all very well, but gave me little clue as to the professional role of each 'foodie,' lurking diffidently behind each waistline. I felt I ought to know, to avoid social gaffe, or worse, surgical error.

First, I tried to make a judgement by considering the amount of paperwork and technological paraphenalia they arrived with. This proved misleading. A rather neat electronic device (could it be for measuring heartbeat?) turned out to be the hand control for my colour TV, and its imposing bearer merely the hospital porter. As he demonstrated the controls, he murmured conspiratorily about the secret whereabouts of mushrooms in my valley.

As my first evening approached, I succumbed to a hedonistic abandonment of the Protestant work ethic that had, in my youth, equated not only toil, but cold, dark bedrooms, with virtue. I welcomed the fading daylight, and rejoiced in anticipating the naughty luxury of bedroom TV. Expecting no further visitors, I eased myself into the warm, indolent pillows and pressed the control button. *King Kong* loomed and boomed, flailed and flickered. Inconceivably, in the midst of this sybaritic bliss, I fell asleep.

A knock on the door awakened me. It was 11.45pm. Two young auxiliaries in blue uniforms entered, to ask if I were comfortably settled down. They offered me an astonishing wealth of nocturnal drinks for the restless insomniac: decaffeinated coffee, cocoa, tea with lemon, tea with milk, and a score of soothing herbal infusions, brewed from the battered stalks and leaves of the most unlikely plants. As I tentatively imbibed a rashly selected green liquid, which tasted faintly of tin, they plumped up my pillows and tucked me up for the night.

Only as they turned to leave did I notice that a pink glow still emanated from the top left hand corner of the room. The TV was still offering its unblinking window on the world. But no longer the world of King Kong, but the shadowy underworld of French TV's '*Série Rose*:' to you and me, soft porn. I vaguely wondered if my quasi-regal status might encourage the girls to back out of the room, thus escaping the Apocalyptic vision of heaving roseate buttocks. My hand fumbled feverishly for the control pack. It slid onto the floor. One of the girls bent down and picked it up. "Have you finished viewing for tonight?" she asked, nonchalently, observing gross phallic improprieties with total gallic unconcern. "I had already had enough. I mean, I never started to watch. That's to say, I **did** start, but that was when the action involved an ape." "Funny preferences, you English," she said. "Good night, and interesting dreams," said the other, closing the door on my confusion.

Next morning another slim, elegant professional in starched white uniform arrived, brandishing a huge questionnaire. I noticed he was wearing disposable plastic gloves, and was confident he must be my surgeon. He spoke of mushrooms, but I had learned by then not to be put off by this, and clung to my theory that he would soon discuss the knife. Indeed, I thought it might be tactful and less embarrassing for him if I gently turned the conversation in that direction. "At home we always have problems chopping musrooms - and meat, for that matter," I said casually, "because I'm a dud at knife-sharpening and slicing." My guest's eyes lit up. He sympathised with me, and assured me it was a veritable art, and required a life-time's professional practice. I felt triumphant in my diagnosis. It was short-lived. With a flourish I was presented with the questionnaire: a huge choice of menus for the meals and wines I would enjoy in hospital. My guest was the chef. "The only slim one in all France," I thought, ruefully.

A pretty girl slid demurely alongside, dressed neatly in a house-coat of romantic mauve, tiny razor delicately poised in tiny hand. Although I rightly surmised, this time, what the purpose of her visit was, and dutifully bared my beleaguered midriff, *et al.*, I was not prepared to be whisked, at such a disadvantage, into a sparkle of discussion befitting a beauty parlour. It was even more surprising, and curiously endearing, to find my work-a-day belly included in her feminine observations. "Ah, you look still young. It is good not to let wrinkles and dryness of skin arrive by getting too *gros* or staying long in the sun. You have also clear skin through eating fruit and yoghurt, *n'est-ce pas?*" "I suppose so," I mumbled, taken aback; then added hopefully, "and local mushrooms." "You climb the mountain often to find them, so are your muscles strong and *ventre* firm: very good for health," she said, gently supporting me with one hand while navigating my nethermost parts with the other. It was civilised not to be treated like a slab of dead meat. But my body and I found it so unusual to receive favourable comment from a stranger, let alone physical attention, that we almost feared untoward reaction. However, the charm of the nurse's eager chatter and her innocent touch disarmed us. All was well, and by common consent our mutual response remained demurely understated.

A cheery, bewhiskered fellow bounced in with an electric monitor tucked under his hairy arm. Another TV technician, perhaps? Wrong again. He slathered gel on my deftly barbered stomach, skated over it with a sort of scanner, and peered absent-mindedly at the monitor screen while talking intently about mushrooms. "After this raining, are many *ceps* in your valley. I must search this weekend my friend '*Henri*. Together we search *ceps*. Also I must search '*Ernie*." "Is he also a friend of yours and a local mushroom expert?" I asked. "*Non, non,* **your** *hernie*, we must find '**eem**!" he said It took me a moment to realise the conversation had swerved into professional mainstream. Here was a radiologist trying to pinpoint the reason for my sojourn in the *clinique*: my elusive hernia.

So considerate was the universal approach, so ineffable my experience, I began to think: "This is no *clinique*, but a four star hotel." I began to fret: Where was the *rigueur* underpinning the *souplesse*? This I knew to be necessary in France, as the bank's training programme had revealed on another occasion, to ensure that the professionals felt they were **being** professional. I had not long to wait.

A stocky, muscular giant knocked and entered the room like a ringmaster. He swung into action with a welter of rubber straps, wires, and plastic suckers. In no time at all I found myself pinned to the bed like a pelt at the tanners. My savagely bound limbs were pitifully spreadeagled north, east, south and west. I was a human weathervane, awaiting the storm. I felt unable to twitch a hair on my chest (a location where they were still extant). Masochistically I succumbed to the gleeful application of the manifold cold and slithery suckers to all parts of my anatomy. Now let the sadist do his worst, I thought, recklessly. For once there was no conversation, as enormous earphones were clapped to his ears. Like a keeper at some hellish zoo, he made his trained octopus do his bidding, tightening every tentacle, - and plugged into the mains.

My pulse raced, my heart pounded. No convulsion, no shock, nothing. "*Impeccable!*" muttered my tormentor. "*Pardon?*" I gasped. "Your 'eart, *impeccable*," he repeated, removing his earphones and loosening my bondage. He called his octopus to heel, strode across the room, and opened the door. As he left, he winked over his shoulder: "Is a fine time for mushrooms."

A nursing sister trotted in, crisp as a biscuit, holding a large feeding bottle. I surmised its liquid contents might be for leisurely imbibing on recovering consciousness, if I were not immediately up to adult mastication. Not so, alas. Although the nurse maximised *souplesse*, the *rigueur* had finally arrived. After delicate entreaty the teat was inserted in an alternative cavity, and the contents of the bottle disgorged. Later there were to be other pills, concoctions, ointments and instruments similarly introduced. Anal insertion as a cure-all is as common a preoccupation of the French medical profession as a shoe-shop is to a foot fetishist. Too late I realised the implications of rarity implicit in the lurid injunction '**VOIE ORALE**', on my medicine bottle, and the look of horror and disgust on Sister's face when I innocently removed a thermometer **from my mouth**.

After the operation the entire hotel staff enquired after my well-being. "*Impeccable*, the recovery of a twenty-five year old," said the surgeon. "There was no swelling after; you will soon be eating mushrooms again." "It was all *gaz*," mused the anaesthetist:"we were **all** nearly anaesthetised." He added: "It may continue for a day or two." "I hope not," said the surgeon fervently. The perfumed mauve-clad *patronne* of the beauty salon, who had previously masqueraded so convincingly as a nurse, opened the window, just in case. Sister, of the alternative baby-feeder, glanced appreciatively at the unplugged cork of my medicine-bottle. She even contemplated ruminatively, it seemed to me, the bunch of sweet-smelling flowers, perilously to hand, on my locker.

Fortunately there was no more *gaz*, and such ready remedies as corks and flowers remain untried, as far as I am aware, even by the French medical profession.

A tale of Eastern promise

During my short stay in hospital and brief convalescence, my student son, who was visiting us on a working holiday with a girlfriend, nobly held the fort with mop and bucket. As they were well received by my loyal customers, and as the business was expanding, I began to wonder whether to employ them part-time on a legitimate basis, for the duration of the season. I resigned myself, with some trepidation, to another full-frontal attack on the *fonctionnaires*.

Little did I appreciate what my proposition would entail, though, knowing rather more by now of French bureaucratic customs, I might have guessed it would not be easy. The girl, of course, was no relation, but judging from my observations of the accomodating French attitude to '*l'amour*,' I did not imagine that would create any problem. How wrong I was. I soon found out that, in her unattached state, the girl failed to qualify as kith or kin (whichever you prefer). This led to the problem proper: nothing I offered to sign would entitle me to take any responsibility for her sojourn in France as accredited *apprentie* while this staus quo prevailed. Since neither partner wished to change status, I decided it was time to seek advice from our multi-talented mayor. If anybody could resolve our difficulties, he could.

The morning of the mayoral interview arrived. The mayor greeted me, stroked his beard reflectively, then said to the girl: "There is but one possible solution which might make your temporary employment acceptable. You must enter forthwith into *concubinage*. It ought to solve any administrative problems, and should make the *fonctionnaires* happy." With some misgivings, the girl hastened to discuss matters with my son, who I think quite relished a role as provisional Sultan. I was somewhat troubled to discover it came all too easy to him to turn his attention to thoughts of the harem. Not that he was prepared to contemplate wearing diaphanous baggy trousers and curly shoes, which was a relief. But then, neither was the girl, which was a pity.

Sons and others

For a while I reflected on events. French verve and nonchalance in simultaneously merging old and new to resolve administrative problems by such astounding devices had quite taken my breath away. But before I had the chance to formulate permanent plans, village life interrupted my urbane cogitations.

My son's girlfriend fell prey to notions of bucolic bliss and ran away with the local goatherd. I was left, 'doing the business' in Whitehall farce style among my stalwart 'townies', ruefully reinforcing their belief that "strange things do allus be besetting Catalonian mountain villages at the time of the full moon, *vous savez.*" Indeed, an untimely return by said goatherd to the town on market day, to buy cheese from his *ex-immorata*, a lass of fiery Mediterranean disposition, resulted in his being pelted with *pâté*, festooned with *fromage*, and downed with a potted duckling, before gendarmes could arrive to place a cordon of road cones around his cowering form. This, incidently, is a common occupation of the local fuzz in the main square of the metropolis, as a modest gesture of public duty. They usually cone off collapsed Renaults, doubled-up Algerian Rap dancers, and the occasional meander of octogenarians, bowed down with glee at the demise of a younger contemporary. This time, it was to protect innocent citizens against the wrath of '*Venus tout à fait a sa proie attachée.*'

Perhaps 'all was for the best in the best of all possible worlds,' not in the sense proffered by Voltaire's aimiable optimists, sitting naively in his satirical target area, but in the context of the imminent panic of an innocent abroad. My tangle with Turkish nomenclature had been sufficient to warn me against too intimate involvement with *fonctionnaires*. Clearly, the allure of relationships appeals to bureaucrats as honey to the bee. When things become personal, nothing better than official access to the hive. They thrive on administration, form-filling, questionnaires and interviews, reducing the time available for the work itself. Moreover, individuals involved in small businesses or the service industries, in proportion to their income or social status, form one of the most highly taxed groups in France. Little wonder that small traders, builders, plumbers and the like, are usually self-employed solo operators, or run businesses limited to members of the family. The fiscal obligations towards an employee 'on the fringe', or outside the family circle, in terms of health insurance and tax contributions are severe. The rule of thumb is that profits disappear the moment you take on staff. State subsidies, benefits and repayments due to the individual suffer Byzantine delays. On the other hand, failure to pay up immediately on demand, on the part of the individual, induces instant penalty. No excuse is tolerated, even a postal strike.

Not surprisingly such official zeal is often self-defeating. The more officialdom tries to stamp out minor irregularities or peccadilloes, the more individuals develop *Système D,* that is, avoiding penalty by devious means. Sometimes people work entirely 'on the black,' though this is becoming increasingly risky. Anonymous *dénonciation*, by irate taxpayers working legitimately, with its overtones of tumbrils and social disintegration, is, sad to say, becoming more common. For me, the incentive to run a legitimate enterprise went hand in hand with respect for my customers. Many were finding life difficult, the recession and growing taxation hard to bear. But they always paid their accounts on the dot. Not only was this a load off my mind as a novice *chef d'entreprise,* but the fact of their prompt payment meant that they recognised that making ends meet might be tricky for me too. Their concern for my success was light years away from my curiosity value as a foreign expat., who perchance had decided to favour France with his wealthy, patronising presence. I was accepted on their own economic terms. I had arrived as an odd stranger; I had become (though still, to be sure, an oddity), to all intents and purposes, one of them. To me, this was the ultimate privilege.

CHAPTER SIX

1000m on a high

'Vive la différence!'

My customers had accepted me; as a window-cleaner, that is. More cautiously, they had come to accept me as an Englishman, much as a small child accepts an elephant. I was a curious, but tolerable, quirk of Nature.

One thing they could not accept was that I chose to live halfway up a mountain at 1000m. "You travel for half an hour to get to work? *Incroyable!*" they admonished, never having heard of commuting. "And you live among sheep at *mille metres? C'est la folie!*"

In vain I explained that the sun also shone on our South-facing balcony, and warmly so, even in mid-winter. In vain I declared that the village boasted twenty-seven year-round residents - some younger than me - as well as a thousand-odd sheep, not to mention goats. To my female customers - 'townies', one and all, - the mountains were only there for the mushrooms; to their husbands, for *la chasse:* autumn preoccupations both. By Christmas, the mountains were definitively a 'no-go' area.

But we knew better. The village had a life of its own, as different from that of the town as chalk from cheese - especially village goat cheese, a delicacy of our mountain Shangri-la.. The first thing to assert is that we were civilized; at 1000m, highly so. In the clear mountain air we boasted a civilization that was, moreover, distinct and rarified. The sound and fury of the cities of the plain arrived breathless and transmogrified. On attaining 1000m the trappings of urban civilisation suffered - if it is not a *reductio ad absurdum* - a sea-change. Take, for example, our first Christmas.

The Mayor the merrier

Great preparations were made to celebrate *Noël* that year. On no account was the local town, *Riberal*, to be allowed to upstage the residents of *Noullogarret*. For a start, we had real sheep. They filled the village street each evening with bleatings for lost lambs, crescendos of skirmishings as each *brebis* ewe was united with her thirsty offspring, every other house a haven, a *bergerie*, a welcome 'room at the inn.'

The greatest achievement was the Christmas tree, cut down by the mayor's own hand from the lofty forest, and painstakingly erected in the carpark, at a respectful distance from the dustbins. In spite of a temporary veto on the street lighting for the whole village, brutally imposed by the electricity moguls, who deemed nothing whatever to be up to safety standards in the entire village, the Christmas tree was duly ablaze. You could feel the heat of the illuminations ten metres away. Red lights, blue lights, yellow lights: no matter; we were all cheered and warmed by this mayoral blaze of independence.

By February, the sheep had long-since gone down to their winter quarters in the valley below. No Christmas decorations remained to clutter the streets and preoccupations of the people down-town. But neither had representitives from the electricity board thought it worth while, as yet, to bring illumination to the streets and inhabitants of our village. No matter. The lights of the mayoral Christmas tree still blazed forth, to lighten the ways and warm the hearts of every villager facing the uncertainties of the 1990s and the stony pathway underfoot.

Lest you imagine that we were entirely beyond the reach, or caring, of metropolitan France, I should point out that television reached us, not as mere couch potatoes, but as participants. We were featured on national TV as an example of a rural village revived, agog with cattle, sheep, trout, and an old goat or two. The village soothsayer and most renowned inhabitant, (she of horticultural propensities), was pictured sitting happily in the sun, with the children of our trout farmer and of the 'other' goatherd on her knee. It is their fathers who, kindness of the EU, have been able to establish their young families in the village, to bring to European dining tables the most excellent fruits of their labour, fresh trout and goat cheese of unparalleled flavour and quality.

A later programme also featured our Nature Reserve, though there is nothing reserved about the villagers' nature. A 'soap' the TV companies did miss out on will serve as an example. The election for mayor, which had so nearly scuppered our request for *cartes de séjour*, came close to scuppering village solidarity, in true metropolitan style. There were dark rumours of intrigue, of commercial and political cartels that would have earned prime time on American TV. It was hinted that the owner of the hydro-electric power plant just beyond the village was providing himself, and an adjacent old flame to boot, with electricity on the cheap. It seemed his crony, the resident mayor, was to be voted out of office because he had moved the village TV booster aerial so that the three of them got good pictures to the exclusion of everybody else except a fourth buddy, the village builder. Now his construction activities had recently taken second place to pig rearing, but, through the mayor's influence, he still won most of the village contracts. Even when the buildings collapsed and had to be converted to pigsties. And each collapsed building purchased for 'agricultural restoration' at what you could only call a' knock-down' price. In the end the mayoral office changed hands without our being able to vote, which was perhaps just as well.

I have already spoken of the new mayor's preoccupation with his cattle. But he has other duties to perform in his role of village headman. Not only does he have to to possess the same skills as every villager, but exercise them in combination, with administrative cunning thrown in. For example, just as he was applying the mayoral stamp to yet another official document on our behalf, an irate villager hammered at the door of the *Mairie* claiming he could not water his beans any more. The mayor rushed up a mountain to see whether the irrigation system had failed and returned nonplussed, since all was in working order. "*Mais non!*" said the Catalan son of the soil, "There's plenty of water, I agree; but now you are tapping the river water as well as the underground spring, it's too warm for my beans."

Another challenge to his virtuosity was the acquisition of a secretary. No problem, you might have thought, as he had already inherited one from the outgoing mayor, fully competent in the ways of word-processors and wordy villagers. The only snag was that, on strict instructions from her medical advisors some two years previously, she was forbidden to do any work at an altitude above 800m. This had suited the ex-mayor, as no commitments could be enshrined in typed memoranda, during his régime, to create embarrassment later. At the same time, he was thought to be full of the milk of human kindness, to boot, insisting she never mount to the giddy heights of the village to do her secretarial duty. The new mayor changed all that. He appointed a replacement. Future mayoral obligations, for good or ill, were to be spelt out. The writing was on the wall. I thought he was a brave man.

A more official mayoral duty was to organise the bicentenary celebrations. According to State decree, these had to take place in front of the War Memorial. Since we were but a tiny village, and all ancestral males had been wily pump politicians and hunters to a man, none had fallen prey to enemy bullets - on either side. *Ergo*, we had no Memorial. Not a bit nonplussed, the mayor decided to make do with the next best thing, and hold the official ceremony in the cemetery.

We stood meekly amid the ancestral village tombs while, girt about in his obligatory *Tricolore*, the mayor made a little speech about revolutions past and present, French and European. We had then to round off proceedings by singing *La Marseillaise*. Since most of the villagers were Catalans, alien national anthems were not in their repertoire. Only my wife and I, Monarchists both, but profiting from a distant wartime *entente cordiale*, could remember the words. As far as I could tell, nobody interred beneath our feet turned over at our sham republican duet.

61

Later, we had a firework display, but they missed a trick by having no Guy. They did look round for an anti-Thatcher Protestant as substitute, but I kept very quiet. We also had a gipsy group to sing and dance to, and lots of *grillade* and *Grenache* wine to go with it. An excellent *soirée*. I could not manage *flamenco,* so degenerated into my usual interpretation of a Scot with a mosquito up his kilt. An old Spanish lady, famous for beans and onions, had sympathised with me for having no daughters. When she saw my Scottish *fandango*, she said it was all for the best, as, clearly, I was *soliste*. Villagers are funny folk. There's not much amiss with my *fandango* as far as I can tell. It usually draws the crowds.

I suppose a behavioural expert would consider dancing to be a tribal rite, as commonplace as tribal costume. To me, however, a novice *Noullogarretois*, cast adrift on a flood-tide of anthropological flotsam and jetsam, what happened was shocking, surprising, and delightful.

Haute couture

High in the Pyrenees, the air is vivid and clear-cut. The language, too, is fanciful but forthright. It follows that fashion exhibits a similar surrealistic common sense.

At the Saturday *soirées dansantes* I have seen old ladies in bedroom slippers and wrap-arounds sporting glittering ear-rings and flowers in their hair; young girls in dungarees wearing high heels and buckles on their shoes; men in shiny dancing pumps and shepherds' cloaks. But, for sheer sartorial splendour, nothing could surpass the *grande dame* I dubbed 'the *Flying Lobster.*'

She appeared on the arm of an old Spaniard - he of the rabbit dung donation - who now sported a flat hat and white, co-respondent's shoes. 'My *cousine*,' he proudly explained, - a useful term for unspecified relationships. Her superstructure was swathed in billowy, scarlet satin. Her blouse had long, loose bat sleeves which effected pincer movements as she swept round the dance floor. She was barnacled with jewellery and sequins, beset by beads and ear-rings. Everything swished sideways, as though she were in the sea. Her lower half was encased in a pair of scarlet pedal-pushers, two sizes too small. Big white buttons chattered like seashells as she attempted the *Cha-cha-cha*, and her feet scuttled along in a pair of green plimsolls. She glistened in the moonlight and clattered up against you from time to time, carried in on a tide of music, causing entanglements and apologies.

Sea fever gripped us all. We whirled in a demented vortex. The 'Flying Lobster' was in the centre, blindfolded, gripping a cushion to her encrusted bosom. When the music stopped, she scampered sideways, placing the cushion at my feet. I looked for sympathy. All tides of compassion had ebbed: mischief was at the flood. I had perforce to clasp her knottily to me, kiss her on both cheeks, and, to a wave of applause, take centre stage.

Cargolade

Village life rises to a crescendo in mid-summer. Dancing and dressing up now take second place to feasting.

You may relish a snail; you may appreciate half a dozen; but four and a half thousand? That is beyond intellectual, never mind gastronomic, absorption. For the English, that is. Not so for the Catalans. The 15th August proves it each year.

Now this is the day on which the Assumption of the Virgin is celebrated. What consumption and Assumption have in common I cannot tell, unless it be for me, a Protestant, a certain queasiness of credulity. For those of unwavering faith, however, the promise of four and a half thousand snails singing *halleluias* on the barbecue was, is now, and ever shall be, a Certitude, an Absolute.

The 15th dawned cloudless, *impeccable*. The ladies of the village assembled in their ennobled '*Centre de Loisirs.*' This constituted a covered yard, equipped with long trestle tables, tucked behind the *Mairie*, and, naturally, overlooking the

Canigou Massif. It boasted a unisex loo and a stupendous view. Both, in time, were to make their appeal felt.

On the tables were heaps of snails. Those in full sun made straight for their brothers in the shade, so the less devoted ladies sat in the sun, idly opening up the snail shells' little front doors and popping a pinch of salt inside. The men, stripped to the waist, fed a large open fire with vine prunings, hurling on top the occasional fragrant *cistus* bush. When the flames had died down, two large iron gates were swung across the ashes, balanced on concrete building blocks left over from the high-rise pig-sty development, and a great tray, the size of our kitchen floor, was set to sizzle, with four and a half thousand snails on board. "When they sing '*halleluia*', they are ready," we were told.

I was prepared to gaze at the *Canigou*, and await the choral *apéritif* with patience and awe. No chance. *Porros*, pointed Catalan flagons of *vin doux* were passed from hand to hand, and you were exhorted to drink deep, holding the *porro* aloft at arm's length, hoping to aim the streaming jet of *muscat* straight down the throat. Too late I appreciated the advantage of being stripped to the waist.

Prompt at midday the snails began to sing, and paper napkins and nails were handed out. It was discreetly done. You could choose the size of nail to suit your appetite and personality. Only the men had rusty nails, which they cleaned surreptitiously on spare chunks of bread. Washing-up bowls full of snails were politely offered round, and you helped yourself to a modest handful or two. A dollop of *ailloli*, garlic mayonnaise, snail and nail at the ready, and the *cargolade* snail-feast began.

After the snails, Catalan sausage, cooked in a huge coil six feet across, and measured by the metre on to your platter. Then pork chops and beefsteaks, washed down with the best *Baixas* regional red wine. Next, *Roquefort* cheese, then the sharp white peaches of the region, their juices pricking like Champagne; then *rousquilles*, the sweet sugared cakes of the region, white as polo mints. And more wine. Much more wine, this time the bubbly *pétillante Blanquette de Limoux*. Finding difficulty in choosing between looking at the magnificent *Canigou* and queuing for the unisex loo. Finding difficulty in speaking French. Then finding no difficulty in it whatsoever.

Late in the afternoon a *sieste obligatoire*. Then back to the leisure centre for a *soirée dansante*. No tables and benches this time, just a disco, a wobbling, whirling central light and everybody - from nine to ninety - dancing. Every now and then a crash of broken glass punctuated the barman's torrent of impatient abuse at finding only one more bottle empty. It applauded his faultless Catalan logic in recognising that broken bottles in the dustbin meant fewer heavy crates to carry when the *fête* was over.

With the wine still flowing freely, introductions seemed easy. A large, beaming, middle-aged man approached, bursting out of a T-shirt on which was emblazoned a purple day-glo racing car and the legend: "*World Champion Chips 88.*" He introduced me to a a fragile old dear of eighty-plus I took to be his mother. "My wife," he said, and spun away, his hand round the waist of a rather younger version. "His daughter?" I hazarded. My toothless neighbour rocked about. "No, his mistress," he cackled. "Doesn't his mother - I mean his wife - object?" "Oh no," my friend explained in careful franglais: "She is *agée* and tired of his bed. The mistress *garde* him there but also *garde* well the old *dame*. Together they live 'appily. He *garde* his shop, the mistress *garde* the shopping and the 'ousework and the wife give the money."

Later I visited the shop in question. A young girl was serving at the counter. "Another mistress?" I joked, on leaving the premises. "Ah yes, and she there also to *garde* his book-keeping," mused my bilingual expert. "I think perhaps too much good thing now." Even for Catalonia.

Web of intrigue

I have mentioned, in passing, the village's pride and joy, its

65

recently founded Nature Reserve. In the high summer, like the *cargolade*, it comes into its own, as I was to discover.

The Catalan countrywoman was crouching by the wayside. In my rear mirror I saw her wave her headscarf urgently. I stopped the van, got out, and asked if I could be of help. "I really don't think so, my dear," she replied, in effortless Home Counties English. "You see, I am gathering spiders for the International Arachnological Convention." She seemed sane, and the headscarf turned out to be a large net. One should be warned of such surprises, I thought, as, mind reeling, I tried to drive home safely.

"Oh yes," said my wife, "it's quite true, and the world is not mad. It is merely that the Head of the Nature Reserve is making a bid for fame, or rather, for the fame of his spiders. Did you realise, there are more varieties of spiders here in our valley than almost anywhere else in Europe?" I should have said, "In that case, why do we have so many summer flies?" but my mind was in neutral, spinning gently.

"How many spidermen, er, spiderwomen, spiderfolk will there be, and where will they stay with all their spiders? *Noullogarret* is pitifully small."

"Oh, there'll be lots of spiderologists - at least fifteen or so, - from all over Europe. They'll be staying here and there with their spiders, in the *gîtes*, in villagers' homes. By the way," she went on airily, "I have offered the organiser our spare bedroom. I doubt if many spiders will scramble through to our room," she added, noticing my bewilderment.

"I'll go and see the mayor," I said. "Surely a convention of animal protectionists, water-diviners, or wild-flower fanciers would have been more *délicat?*"

"You can't go to the *Mairie*," my wife said, shaking her head. "That's where they're studying their spiders - unless you have a spare microscope to lend them. There's an unfortunate lack of high tech. in the village, it seems. Oh, and as for your other daydreams, they are to be fulfilled. There's to be an excursion up the mountain to count marmots, and some young people are coming to open up the Nature Reserve pathway, designed to illustrate how much the original villagers depended on water for their welfare; indeed, at every step they took through life."

"So does a window-cleaner," I mumbled, but she didn't hear.

"These events will be rounded of with a slide lecture on wild flowers. What more could you wish for?" she said, triumphantly. "I've put you down for all three activities."

To conclude. The spiderologists spidered their way up to, into, and down from our hapless village, caught like a fly in the spinning webs of international spiderdom. My impotence in the matter was inadvertently wished upon our resident spiderman, who, in a fit of arachnological exhuberance, offered to share his allotted single bed with a keen spiderwoman. My anarchistic son and friends placed an inflatable plastic whale from our swimming-pool in the bed, as a mark of their preference for the 'Save the Whale' campaign to any form of spider conservation. There was not enough room for three in the bed, nor was there room for the whale beside it. It was too large, when inflated, to be thrust through the door, and in the dark neither spiderphile could find the valve to let the air out. Throughout the night, judging from the stifled giggles nudging through the wall, the couple were doubled-up more with hilarity than passion.

My British pride to the fore, I went up the mountain to count marmots. I thought we were staying overnight in the mountain refuge. I was the only person so misled, and thus the only person without a tent. The Head of the Nature Reserve nobly invited me into his, an ex-commando effort designed for one very fit, very thin soldier. We passed a tense but tactful night, with no references made to spiderlovers' clandestine couplings - or whales - though that story had been the talk of the convention.

At dawn we rose, gingerly, bones and muscles creaking in unison. We split into our eight watches, pens, paper and calculators at the ready. Binocular lenses were polished, and we urgently studied the questionnaire. It was earnest, erudite and optimistic. In essence, quite impracticable. It even demanded we try to work out family relationships between the marmots observed. I waited. I went on waiting. I saw not a single marmot. My son and his friends, choosing a viewpoint close to the wine flagons, saw fifteen.

Meekly accepting a humbler role, I joined the pathfinder team. I tugged at trees and rummaged meaningfully among roots and boulders, releasing a buried spring. Suddenly I was ankle-deep in Nature Walk mud, which I suppose proved the sociological point.

Later, the youngest little girl helper cut a blue, white and red tape and the pathway was declared officially open by the mayor, with much ceremony and even more *muscat* to follow. I found myself in amiable conversation with him about the slide lecture on mountain flowers, which was to round off the evening. No spiders, not even a cobweb in the corner of the room, were mentioned.

Mellow with *muscat*, I attended the lecture without mishap, only falling asleep during the second half.

"The Nature Reserve will bring you *la tranquillité*," says the booklet, soporific with fey illustrations of flora and fauna enjoying the mountain sunshine.

I'm still waiting.

Close encounters of the fundamental kind

The following year, no doubt arranged to coincide with the Olympic Games, our local Nature Reserve determined to excel in its choice of study programmes for sporty Nature buffs. Spiderology as a topic I had thought ill-advised, as I knew many folk approaching *le troisième age* of retirement whose eyes sparkled anew on entering our *petit paradis*. Privately they acknowledged that they were inspired by the frisky mountain air to renew their study of Nature's ways. In particular, because they had unlimited time at their disposal in which to become proficient, they deemed it not too late to take a back to basics refresher course on the behaviour of the birds and the bees, if such were available. For them, spiders were an anti-climax. Ever an optimist, I awaited this year's programme with bated breath.

The announcement was made. The study was indeed a basic one, but so fundamental as to discourage all elderly romantics and all but the most stalwart scientists. Only those with an unswerving nose for Nature signed up. The aim of the course was to collect, collate, and correlate: droppings.

I realise that you can learn much of Nature's lore by recognising signs: footprints in the snow, the song of a bird hidden in a thicket, the grunting of the invisible nocturnal beastie. Memories remain vivid of Adventure Books for Boys where a docile Christian Red Indian would save a brave British hunter from wolves or worse by tracing *spoor*, but the delicacy of the authors forbade precision. No Redskin or Army Subaltern ever admitted to unparalleled skill in the investigation of turds. Crapologists, in a nutshell, went unrecognised by the Empire.

Modern French biologists, however, are made of sterner stuff. First, their intrepid leader apologised for running the course out of season, where life in the Great Outdoors at 1000m was cold enough, I would have thought, to induce terminal constipation. He explained that, at any other time of year, flies could be somewhat intrusive. I remembered my son-of-the-soil experience with the rabbit dung donated by the *Flying Lobster's* cousin, and heartily concurred. Up and down the icy mountainsides the teams scurried, *ventre à terre*, as it were, lovingly popping the objects of their research into plastic bags, for closer inspection, or, as a true scientist would more accurately say: 'analysis.' All day long they stooped and scooped. Immune to rural mockery, at evening they returned turd-laden, but undeterred, to the village.

The subject of their study may have been rudimentary, but their methods were high-tech. To freeze and dry out their samples, or *crottes*, they borrowed a fridge from one unsuspecting housewife, and from another, a micro-wave. They sniffed, dissected, identified, and sniffed again The idea was to examine the eating habits of small mammals living in the valley, such as squirrels, badgers, marmots, civet cats, and foxes. Triumphant claims were made for for the more voluminous and exotic rectal treasures. One participant rejoiced in having doubtless found the excreta of wild boar - identified by "the way it glistens!" Another needed both hands to uphold his claim that a rare, but large, mountain deer had previously paused on the path he had later fortuitously trod. He was upstaged by a third, claiming that a heaven-sent evacuation he had stumbled upon was the offering of a lynx. Not one, but two turds, each perfectly formed, clinched it, he avowed. Fortunately, since the Nature Reserve's laboratory is quite small and airless, residues of the larger mammals were infrequently recuperated. Nonetheless, I took comfort from the assertion that there had been no elephants hereabouts since Hannibal.

A further refinement has been to produce a *crotte* recognition handbook. It is loose-leaf, I can't imagine why, and printed on pink paper.

Birds of passage

In *Noullogarret*, as I have mentioned, the summer crescendo is amplified by the arrival of non-residents. By our third year, we were neither immune nor wholly blameless.

Have you ever wondered, sitting on a suitcase at Gatwick, just where everyone else is going?

Well, while you're toying with your brainwave for a suitcase designed to sit on - with built-in cushioning, fold-out arms, retractable back-rest even - I'll tell you: they're off to our little Catalan hide-away. "Not true," you say. But it is, because I'm there when it happens, to prove it.

First to arrive that summer was a composer, in a decomposing Ford. Or rather his distrait entourage of wife and children arrived. He was stranded half a kilometre down the mountain trying to persuade his conveyance it was in the home stretch. The car would have none of it, and our purposeful, all-purpose mayor had to be called out. (All French mayors are purposeful, but *polyvalent* ones are rarer, and much to be valued.). He duly turned up, with a grin and a hammer, and quickly knocked life and locomotion into the vehicle.

Meanwhile the composer composedly took off all his clothes (except for a panama hat), acquired my bathing trunks by sleight of hand, and waded absent-mindedly to the epicentre of my little round swimming-pool. He stood there, very still, for an hour or so. The outcome was a cantata and a cantankerous family who wanted tea.

Next on the scene were a handsome, well-dressed couple from Amsterdam, for whom Holland had fallen a little flat. They claimed they had come for the mountain views and balmy breezes. The first thing they did was to don smelly sweaters and disappear underground, crawling through tunnels and stumbling over stalagmites all night long. They emerged a little demented and a lot deformed.

Then there was the student who came on a working holiday, aspiring to help me clean windows for a while, during the summer rush of work. On tiptoe she could barely reach the sills. Lest this should betray a lack of professional *hauteur*, she had equipped herself with an extending ladder and a long pole. The pole was forever falling down before her, as if smitten with subservience. To avoid being spotted as a holiday-maker, she sought anonymity within a colossal pair of dungarees, which she flaunted like a banner to artisanal solidarity. During the sacred *heure de repas*, spent on the shore of a nearby lake, she would curl up in them like a *croissant*, and go to sleep. Sometimes the warmth would entice her from her sartorial crysalis, to bask in the sunshine, comely and unencumbered.

A wild-eyed pork butcher turned up straight from a kibbutz, betrayed by philanthropy into bankruptcy. He awaited transcendental revelation and a cheque from his aunt in Worksop.

There was the writer who made notes on everything he saw and everything he did. When he was seeing nothing or doing nothing he made notes on his notes. His wife was an artist, who made huge sketches in a huge sketchbook, intending to take them home and make tiny drawings from them.

I warmed instantly to the benevolent Brits. who came on a cycling holiday. They tried so hard to do everything the French way, kissing us and embracing us at every opportunity. Sadly, the opportunities were rare, as they had their mounts seemingly affixed to their persons most of the time, which put them at a physical disadvantage.

The quartet up the road were pally, too, with A married to B, with no child in the offing; and C unmarried to D, with offspring much in the onning. With consummate care, I'm glad to say, our friendship remained intact.

Intriguing were the Planners. They spent an hour each day over breakfast, and two hours making sandwiches. They pored over maps and guidebooks, then scurried hither and thither, piling up little hills of galoshes, sunglasses, rain-hats, sandwiches, binoculars, dictionaries, suncream and mufflers. Ants came to mind, and admiration for the Planners' forethought. Yet the moment they opened the boot of their car, parked some distance from the house, activity ceased. They bowed over the abyss meekly, solemnly, as if in prayer. Time stood still. Then they scampered back to the house again, carrying their little bundles, depositing some, returning with others. They finally got in the car and drove off - without their sandwiches.

In contrast, our friendly professor of languages from Berlin, he of the grosse *Bohrmaschine*, displayed the quiet discipline and Teutonic determination of *Vorsprung durch Technik*. He was a Green, and an intellectual one at that. What more appropriate than to try *"Annihilating all that's made / To a green thought in a green shade"* by uprooting native rock plants and erecting a barricade of conifers on his frontier. The shade, alas, never materialised, as the delicate conifers shrivelled in the sun by day, and were nibbled by goats by night. "Never mind," he said ruefully, "it's the thought that counts."

His Parisian companion had meanwhile adopted a more urbane way of keeping cool: the shower. What intrigued me was that, no matter what hour of the day I knocked at their door, she would always emerge, sleek as a seal, streaming with water, not allowing her towel, wafted vaguely in the direction of her bosom, to impede her expansive gestures of welcome. Eyes shining, she would say "Always it is pleased to see, *n'est-ce pas?"* It was.

One day we had an apparition on our doorstep. He wore collar and tie, with cuffs buttoned at the wrist, no matter the ambient temperature, like a Victorian sahib. His face was a still-life in off-white and eggshell. It emerged he was *Brain of Britain*, whereat the thought struck me he might render a small service. Knowing I would be away from home for a short time I asked him to fix a hasp on a cupboard door. I returned to find the cupboard agape - and no hasp. The *Brain* explained, with unnerring precision: "I regret it was not done, though I gazed at the problem from every angle and every side for several days."

Once we found installed a solid, squarish fellow who, since retirement, had run a personalised car hire service for VIPs attending formal functions at the Savoy, and informal rendez-vous in Shepherd's Market. Clients arrived, or failed to arrive, at Heathrow, or Stansted. He waited. And now, aloft in the Pyrenees, eyes focussed at infinity, he sat, embedded in his armchair like the Sphinx in the sands of Time I realised he wasn't relaxing: he was waiting, as usual. Gatwick and Godot were his addiction.

A fresh-faced director of the Pru., unaccustomed to the mountain road, rolled up in a fresh Jaguar and a fresh sweat.

With him was a fresh wife. How he enjoyed the flowers, the streamlets, the sunshine: beginning life afresh in the fresh mountain air.

One unwelcome visitor we called '*King Kong's Auntie.*' When she couldn't sleep, she rose up in rage and broke things: like shutters, taps and pendulums, whose nocturnal small talk bothered her.

Delightful, but disturbing, was the lepidopterist who would nonchalantly head for a precipice when making a bee-line, so to speak, for a butterfly, casually disregarding those in our stomachs.

Then there was *Tinky*. That wasn't her real Christian-name, but nobody knew what that was, and all agreed she seemed to have no need of a surname. Her forte was baths, beds and breakfasts. All were approached late, leisurely, and lasted long. No-one ever knew whence she came, why she came, or when she departed.

Nor should I forget the entire family who came for a rest-cure and stayed to renovate a ruin - the key to getting their castle in the air off the ground: ten years' hard labour.

We had an author, whose hand so often held a pen that he never dug it into his pocket. To make amends, his companion took him in her stride on healthy walks before dinner, admiring vast vistas and preparing vast pizzas.

For a time the entire valley lay in the shadow of a huge Slovak and his enfolding Hanoverian wife. He made music the way others make mayhem. The valley rang with canons forged from Catalan - like cannon forged from the *Canigou*. His music didn't just make the world go round: it made it go round fast and furious.

There was an old colleague from student days who turned up from New Zealand unexpectedly and turned our lives upside-down for an afternoon of topsy-turvy déjà-vu.

But most I remember the children.

William, all of fifteen, bronzely and brazenly lazing on his back in the pool on an inflatable crocodile. Illicit beer in hand, he gazed up at the giggling French teen-age talent from what they knew, but pretended not to know, was a delectably illicit angle.

Three year old Christopher, promising never to pee in his pants again if he could be allowed to ride up the cloudless valley in the little yellow train.

Thomas, seven, for whom every rock was vivid with vipers and adventure.

And eleven year old Becky, for whom the mountains spelt mystery; where the morning skies shimmered with old tales and present imaginings; and where the evening mists merged into the yearning for that marvellous tomorrow that is every young girl's birthright.

One day, suddenly, the swallows had gone, and with them our other summer visitors. The lambs were bleating again in their winter quarters next door, their cries like those of happy children gone back to Gatwick. It was hard to believe next year they'd be back, heaven forbid: thank God.

CHAPTER SEVEN

Talk of the town

Of dogs and ducks and dinner-time

In the mountains, I had come to learn that *la tranquillité* could be evasive. In the town, too, where work ceases for all on the stroke of noon, the hallowed sequence of midday meal and siesta, *repas et repos*, could, on occasion, be desecrated.

It is true that lunchtime in the main square of *Riberal* is usually quiet and peaceful. *La tranquillité* even affects service in the *Brasserie de L'Univers* which borders it. Waiters take their time over orders, chat to friends, drop a glass or two, and make mistakes adding up bills. Nobody seems to mind too much, except a couple of overweight tourists from Munich with an itinerary to keep to. They flap their maps and guidebooks and sweat and expostulate, but to little avail. *C'est l'heure de repas,* and they do not realise that everyone hereabouts takes two.

Today, however, was different. I sat outside the *Brasserie de L'Univers*, in my favourite corner, sandwich in one hand, a beer in the other, ladder and bucket set aside. It had been an energetic morning, and I was glad of a sit-down.

Things began quietly enough. A little old lady with her *chien de poche* as conversation-piece wandered amiably across the square and sat down near the central fountain to chat about her dog and its day to an ageing hippy. He was sitting, backed up against the fountain in its shade, legs splayed out before him like a huge yawn. A length of frayed, dirty string linked him loosely to a huge wolf of a dog. Its flanks were quivering and its eyes, cruelly blue, were looking for action. The hippy had something tucked away in the recesses of his leather jerkin, which bulged and wobbled darkly.

Two small girls in pretty summer dresses crossed the square to the fountain. Aged about seven or eight, they were attracted by the spray and the cool basins. They plunged their hands in, then started flipping water over each other. They giggled and splashed some more. They shot a look at an upper window, where their mothers were doubtless enjoying a *digestif* after lunch. They called a truce, took off shoes and socks and dresses and placed them carefully out of splash range. Then they began water games in earnest, chasing each other round and round the fountain, splashing and shrieking with laughter. Finally, quite abandoned to their summer delights, they took off their pants, threw them onto their pile of clothes -   just missing the old lady - climbed together into one of the basins, and jumped up and down, squealing.

All this time the wolf was becoming more and more agitated. Suddenly, out of the shadows wandered three old woofters, one of whom was *César*, famed elderly watch-dog of the adjacent *Rue de la Cordonnerie*. Off bolted the wolf, snatching the string out of the sleepy hippy's grasp. Like a fiend from Hell he rounded up the three old-stagers, snapping and snarling at their heels, as he drove them in *troika* formation about the fountain. They skidded and clawed their way in a crazy circle of spurting dust and grit, like demented speedway aces. Eyes bulging, jaws agape, they sped round and round, too frightened to bark. Nevertheless, the racket in the square reached pandemonium pitch as the *chien de poche* yelped loud enough for fugitives and avenger alike.

It was then that one of the mothers looked out of her window and saw the naked daughters huddled terrified in the basin, two *Graces* in disgrace. "Get out! Put your clothes on! And come here this minute!" she shouted. But fearful and tearful, cut off from all access to modesty and rehabilitation by a snarling welter of hounds, they dared not, could not.

Finally, the three dogs rushed off up the *Rue de la Cordonnerie*. The hellish circuiting was broken, the girls sobbed their way into the shadows of maternal wrath, the wolf returned laconically to his master, the *chien de poche* stopped having hysterics, and peace was restored to the square.

A short while later, two crestfallen little girls, demurely dressed once more, walked hand in hand across the square up to the lady with the carried dog, to apologise. Even in the *Midi*, mayhem and immodesty demand a restorative touch of *la politesse*, to maintain the civilised balance of *la vie française*. That goes for children and adults too.

The hippy, amused at the decorous pair, finally bestirred himself to reveal what was hidden in his jerkin: a little fluffy duckling. The little girls were enraptured, stroking it and encouraging it to waddle for a paddle towards the forbidden fountain. Realising that such a development might cause a repetition of parental ire, the hippy stood up, tied the wolf to a bollard, and led the little group, including the old lady with her carried dog, up the *Rue de la Cordonnerie*.

At this time of day the gutters are flushed with water to wash away the dust and detritus of the morning. The idea was for the girls to put the duckling in the water upstream, so that it could paddle safely down to where its owner awaited it. What a thrill for the girls, to be present at the very first swim of a duckling's life: a Great Aquatic Adventure. In the porch of his home, *César* rested, recovering from his own Great Vulpine Adventure. He cocked a bushy eyebrow at the goings-on.

The duckling was launched, and was swept revolving giddily downstream at a terrifying rate. The girls ran after him, shouting for the hippy to be ready. Too late. The duckling shot past and plunged ever more quickly downstream towards a gaping drain. The girls shrieked in terror. Suddenly *César* jumped up and bounded after the retreating object, a bobbing black and yellow duster about to dust no more. *César* overtook the doomed duckling. He leaped into the water. He took up the duckling in his jaws. More terror! Would *César* now crunch him up as *hors d'oeuvre?* It was long after his dinner-time, and he had had a very trying day so far. But no; this mongrel with no perceptible pedigree retrieved the duckling from the ditch, carried it carefully in his jaws without biting, and laid it dutifully at the hippy's feet, a retriever to the manner born. The little girls, the hippy and the old lady, and, for all I could tell, her carried dog too, hugged one another in delight, and fussed and patted *César* no end.

César, however, was not pleased. He wanted the hippy to hurl the duckling down the street, so that he could race after it again, and, panting, bring it back. When all was said and done, he was only a mongrel who wanted to play ball.

The haven where they would be

Normally, however, midday is a quiet time, and the French brasserie the epicentre of *la tranquillité*. Downtown in *Riberal*, one is *primus inter pares*.

If you're a tourist feeling a little sea-sick with the ups and downs of sight-seeing, the tos and fros of finding bakeries not breadless, and the ins and outs of cashing travellers' cheques, you probably think you deserve a drink. The Catalans are wiser. A watering hole is not enough. What is needed is an anchorage where ambience is all. Follow in the wake of most downtown journeymen at *midi* and you'll find yourself headed towards the *Brasserie de L'Univers*, a veritable haven.

It is well-named, for in the outer roads the flotsam and jetsam of many nations bob and dip alongside the welcoming white tables and chairs. Brazenly, apologetically, or inadvertently, German, English and Dutch tongues flap and fly the flag. Their owners squint in the too-bright sun at their daring drinks.

Not so the canny skippers. They moor in the inner harbour by the bar. Its lights flash on and off, but it's not a nautical signal - just an electrical overload. A raffish privateer, or so you imagine, heaves to. He sports dark glasses and a wide-boy fifties jacket. His sultry moll jangles with jewellery. They pore over a newspaper quiz promising a fast buck and a holiday for two in the *Antilles*. But there's no skullduggery after all. He is a respected banker.

Jetting up to the landing stage a golden boy with locket and floral shirt plays a one-armed bandit for all he's worth, a flotilla of pretty girls in tow. A professional gambler? Well, not exactly: just your friendly next-door insurance agent, for once taking his own chances.

Next coasts in to a discreet corner table a stately pair, dressed overall. Slowly they reef in billowy summer coats, scarves floating like bunting. His proud face is a figure-head, deliberately turned so that it is seeen only in profile. She, having pecked at a menu, settles her face, brown and smiling, on her bosom, as happy and hopeful as a hen upon eggs. A high street jeweller, she is used to counting chickens.

An old man chugs by, with a waistband like a lifebelt. All expression is battened down under a flat cap. But his eyes are on the alert, swivelling to see who is harbouring the daily paper. Once he has it, he, too, will tie up at the bar, rocking gently from side to side as he reads.

A sleek black shiny young man from *Réunion*, his sleek black shiny dog chained alongside, cuts a dash through family groups moored at their midi tables. They nod *Bonjour* as he turns about. An ancient wallows near the bar. Her beachcombing eyes, agog for discarded beer, gleam like ship's lanterns. A gulp here, a swallow there, and she drifts surreptitiously away, her hair wild and loose, untrimmed to the winds of change.

Just inside the bar, but looking outward, focussing on horizons way beyond the bobbing skyline of tourists, is a bearded Dutch *emigré*. *Pastis* in hand, he dreams. What is he - or was he? A writer, an ageing hippy, maybe the only true sailor? He - but don't we all? - quickens to her spicy perfume as *la patronne* darts in amongst us, new push-chair bouncing in her wake. We ripple in respect. Young and spirited, she glances appreciatively around, then sets sail again with unselfconscious grace. All eyes follow. The waiters, clumsy or adroit, weave among the *clientèle*, and waver, their bills unnoticed and unpaid.

But it is time to weigh anchor. Nice to know *Riberal* - of all seas, the most buoyant.

English as she is bespoke

Do you remember hula hoops? If so, mock not the French, whose latest craze is to possess *Un Pin's*. It is not wise to ask how the apostrophe got in there. According to the *patron of Chez Pierrot*, it has been inserted to avoid confusion with the *argot* for the male member; in effect a last-ditch attempt by the *Académie Francaise* to uphold, by desperate differentiation, the fading nobility of the French language. But that's his story, to be shared conspiratorily with his window-cleaner.

But if no-one takes the language seriously any longer, *pin's* are a different matter altogether. They are to be taken as seriously as *midi*, and twice as seriously as Mitterand. Without at least five of these cheeky little enamelled metal nuggets of Advanced Art smirking on jacket, shirt, blouse or blouson, you are sartorially naked, and *pas sortable* - not fit to be seen out with. They feature sports, animals, motor cars, pop singers, spacemen, flags, logos and emblems of all kinds. Of course, you have to pay huge sums for *pin's* for personal adornment. For what advertising cannot afford to achieve by purchase, it obtains by selling. Very logical: very French.

But the psychological reason for the whole population's amassing *pin's* as squirrels amass nuts remains, from the General Public's point of view at least, as obscure as the intrusive apostrophe. Doubtless those responsible for making a fashion of subliminal subterfuge know all about it; but I have learned it is rash to interrogate French advertising executives, and ruinous to question French grammarians.

Pin's, on the whole, are a winter obsession. In summer, grammatical and sartorial couplings in the interests of brainwashing the populace take a different turn.

August is the apogee of tourist-time. In Catalonia pride and blood-pressure mount with the temperature. Handbills are thrust through doorways. Notices are stuck up on every window I try to clean. One in particular caught my eye as I grappled with sticky-tape and exasperation. It read:

"France sets a high target for education by the year 2000. The Education Commission would like to see a strong emphasis on foreign languages, with language studies beginning at primary school level throughout the country."

It is true that failure to grasp the rudiments of the language of the country you are in can be disconcerting. From my own experiences, I could well sympathise with an Catalan farmer who was invited to attend the Lancashire wedding of a daughter of an elderly friend of mine, a retired manageress in the clothing business, whom he had frequently driven to market. Taking fastidious objection to his weather-beaten pullover on the Great Day, as she was about to introduce him to the pair of nubile bridesmaids, she poked at the garment and said "Teck it off!" Thinking this was the polite way to go about English introductions, he fingered one of the girls' bodices and repeated, as best he could "Teck eet off," bowing and smiling broadly.

Pondering on such events, and on the high-minded, patriotic ambition of the written announcement, I wondered how the populace of a small provincial town like ours might be expected to react to the challenge. I was soon to find out. The secret weapon was to be sartorial.

On my next visit to market I kept my eyes open and what did I see? Every T-shirt, every sweat-shirt, every *blouson* boasted a portable English lesson. No matter the size or design of garment, whether intended for toddler or octogenerian, slender teen-age sex-pot or pot-bellied toper, phrases in English hit you in the eye and jockeyed for attention. The directive to tailors from the Education Department was clearly: "Write it colourful and write it large." It was to be memorable, rather than meaningful. I cite a few examples, to illustrate the earnestness evident in each endeavour, not flinching at grammatical approximation, where imagination may otherwise lose out.

Authentic Styl featuring the World's Greating. L Royalty's Trade Mark: Guard Coast

Sweet Sea Light at Pretty Little Faces.

*American Feeling and Appreciation, / USAF Navigator /
RAF Air Paradise Major*

*At 10am the 5th November 1945 a spitfire fall down
beside line,(Secret)*

*Once upon a time a little boy who had two fishes and for
house a boat to Flipper's*

*Nov 1823 a marb is inscription as the English School of
Rugby commemorates the birth of the sport*

*The Amazing old good time / Good time to appreciate all
the value of 'American Dream' / That is the symbolism of
new technologies and new economical views*

Famous memories / We keep challenging/ New and Basic

*Air Voyager North South / In every important occasion
take the plane*

*Highness Empress divine / For ever a loyal subject in your
Kingdom*

Hog dog / Coco by Sweaty

Happy Smiles'

Further comment on this worthy endeavour to wed fashion to
phraseology would, I think, be superfluous. The merits of
'Designer Education' are self-evident, and may be inferred *sans
paroles.*

All the fun of *l'affaire*

With the *météo* forecast on a high, what better than a fair to
justify the thermometer's dizzy climb? Another good reason to
down bucket and ladder.

In France fairs are taken seriously. Like business. Or fun. They
draw together, for a precious moment in time, the counter-
valent forces of State and Citizen; *fonctionnaire* and street

trader. Politics and commerce cohabit with extrovert, though temporary, *panache*.

Gendarmes arrive in force and new striped uniforms. Their motorcade gleams and weaves through the gathering crowd like a shoal of mackerel. Streets are cordoned off, cars excluded from the charmed circle where all comers are to be sucked into an instant whirlpool of Official Fun. An appointed band duly strikes up, but the blanket of State decorum is airily tossed aside by the exhibitionist music. Tangos replace military marches. *La Vie en Rose* replaces *La Marseillaise*. Pretty local girls in mini-skirts unfurl in amateurish abandon professional stickers of national banks, insurance agencies and newspapers, their long legs enticingly entangled in the po-faced publicity. Coloured banners billow in the town square like an armada eager to set sail. If the girls could follow the swirling motorcade - sirens, horns and hooters blaring - they would.

Seek out *Brasserie de L'Univers* and you choose between the Waltzers and the Dodgems. Lights flash on and off in the copper-clad ceiling. I know they always did, but this time it surely has to be in honour of the eddying current of men of affairs: journalists, TV producers, local politicians and businessmen. Fans and fanatics, they bump their way between tables to the bar, or rotate where they stand, glass in astonished hand.

Suddenly the *raison d'être* flashes into view. The national heroes of the *Tour de France* blur by to tumultuous applause. They shine and spin in the sun. Then they are no more. The sailing banners are furled, the sirens stilled, the girls gone. The citizens are set free from Official Fun. But there's enough *muscat* over for them to start making their own. *Vive La Révolution. Vive La France!'*

'Let them eat cake!'

On non-feast days, the casual onlooker wandering downtown might surmise that Catalan commercial activity had gone into reverse. Shops would delight in sticking a notice in their windows saying *'congé annuel'* or *'fermature exceptionelle'*. To those with a smattering of French this was puzzling, as the shops never seemed to open at all.

As a window-cleaner, I was privileged to learn at first hand what lay behind such apparent lassitude. Hard-nosed commercial acumen, that's what. The first notice was a blind, nothing to do with annual holidays. It simply meant that the owner had retired and the shop was up for sale. During negotiations to purchase, a little commercial decorum was deemed fitting. The second announcement was subtler still. Certainly it soon became obvious that there was nothing exceptional about the closure: such shops were closed most of the time. The puzzle was to find out why. Again, my access to my clients as a simple *artisan* was to help me to unlock the secret.

Surprisingly, to excel as a Catalan *commerçant*, or trader, you must keep your shop closed for most of each day. In spite of protesting queues outside the door, it must remain closed, sporting its exasperating little notice, as often and for as long as possible.

To a mere Englishman, for whom wartime restrictions are a distant memory, this approach may seem counter-productive, to say the least. Not so. And I have evidence to prove it.

As humble *nettoyeur*, I was bidden to present myself at a certain baker's shop at 4pm sharp, to undertake the necessary cleaning of the enterprise, reputedly the most prosperous in town. At five-to-four, the blinds remained drawn, the door firmly locked. A long queue had formed outside, muttering, as all queues do, about Life and Fate and the Universe. To be more precise, about the justification for a *baguette* to have a recurring place in their universe. At four o'clock precisely, a beaming *patronne* flung open the door. By four-fifteen, she was sold out, and a different notice went up: *'Plus de pain'* - 'no more bread.'

On other Mondays in summertime, when the *sieste obligatoire* tended to extend itself ever further into the afternoon, this nonchalant triumph was was even more finely judged: open at 4.10, closed at 4.15pm. I hardly had time to twirl my leather.

As my acquaintanceship grew less breathless, I determined to find out how on earth she made a success of this 'now-you-see-it, now-you-don't' bread business. "Why don't you stay open longer?" I asked her, innocently. She looked at me in scorn. *"Mon Dieu*, and make my poor husband rise earlier to make more bread? He would become soon *fatigué* and make what you say lousy bread, so no-one buy it, even if I stay always open. We make little. We make good. We sell all."

"What if customers come and you are closed already?" I ventured. *"Tant pis!"* - too bad - she shrugged. "There is supermarket always open to buy stale *croissants."*

CHAPTER EIGHT

That's the way to do it

Beauty is in the 'Aye!' of the beholder

Feasts and fairs are fine in their way. The memory lingers on - but for how long? As I was to discover, plying my humble trade, election time demands more permanent mementos.

Whenever a local election is announced, every councillor is stricken with a passion for Advanced Art. The office of the local editor of the regional paper is suddenly aglow with vast paintings whose talent pants breathless in the wake of their inspiration. Children's prize-winning drawings bedeck the *Riberal Mairie* annexe like bunting, and posters advertising exhibitions jostle for attention in every shop window. Without first responding to the messages, then looking over, under, or round them, you can't rightly tell the butcher's from the baker's. The purpose is simple: the Council must not only do things, but be seen to be doing things, as publicly as possible. And what more fitting for candidates in the painters' *Midi Paradise* than to be made visible and vote-worthy through Sponsored Art?

That year, however, the Mayor and his entourage opted not only for art but for architecture also: prettiness ubiquitous; politics made permanent; our mini-metropolis itself the unhidden persuader.

Urgently requested to wash down the forecourt of a notable block of apartments near the church, I sensed something unusual was afoot. First they had dug up the road to put in new drains. Nothing unusual - even if rare - in that. But then they had replaced your normal tarmac with bricks in blushing rose-pink, clearly intended to dazzle the eye and disarm the voters. Our metropolitan mayor, however, is made of sterner stuff. He wanted to create a truly indelible impression. Great cast-iron globes in marine green suddenly appeared in the historic *Rue*

Wifred le Velu, anchored haphazardly to parking bays, carriageways and pavements. Indelible impressions were rapidly made - mostly on car bumpers - as drivers tried vainly to negotiate the rotund pustules. It was a minefield with only roadsweepers, not minesweepers, to hand.

Lest an unwanted element of counter-productivity should sidle into the minds of those paying hefty repair bills at the nearest garage, an article extolling the ineffable beauty of the globes appeared in the local press, with a photograph of the mayoral inauguration of *le chromatisme de Wifred* . The style was one for all seasons, and the colour-scheme professionally chosen, it was claimed, to match certain columns in the *Louvre*. Only the patina was missing, and time would surely see to that. Their permanent utility was also carefully explained: to separate motorist from pedestrian. This was hardly necessary, as the motorists were mostly anchored in the nearest garage forecourt, while pedestrians, nursing bruised shins and broken toes, were hove to in adjacent hospitals or hostelries.

More eye-catching still is an arty erection abutting a row of sedate 19th century terraced houses, also near the town centre. The nautical theme is maintained, for the construction has the over-generous girth of the stern of a Channel ferry, painted pink with a red taffrail. Its purpose is obscure, except to local cats who prefer rehearsing there to performing on a row of dustbins opposite. Perhaps it is a band-stand, or rather, half a band-stand, for its shape is but semi-circular. Perhaps it is a stab at the baroque ultimate in Speakers' Corner soapboxes, for there has to be a vote in it somewhere. It holds up the traffic while holding our attention. Perhaps that is all that is needed.

They have also been busily beautifying the church door. At first it retained the natural look of warm, sandy, rough-hewn stone, blending modestly into the 17th century stonework of the church. But as such it caused not a blink of attention. Something had to be done. The stonework was sand-blasted smooth and painted a dazzling white. Perhaps those entering by this portal are not to be too distracted from attending mass: merely reminded subliminally (nothing crude in his artful campaign) that the mayor's name is implicit in the colour chosen.

'We shall remember them'

As October shakes out its winter woollies, a-bobble with *la fantaisie*, and I remember to keep my water hot, chrysanthemum time comes round again. These lovely flowers are only used in France as commemorative blooms to put on graves (forgotten for the rest of the year) at the time of All Souls. As usual in these parts, it is an excuse for a feast, and there is a rush to provide the market with oysters in equal over-abundance. Chrysanths teeter on the *trottoirs* in tier after tier, while oysters topple from road-side trays, high as the Tower of Pisa, but less vertical.

I was walking along, minding my own - or rather some dog's - business tenaciously attached to my shoe. A road-tanker was approaching, its driver engaged in the crazy economic logic of transporting a huge load of petrol to *Andorra* for motorists to purchase at a premium, divide into little loads and bring all the way down again. He panicked at the sight of an unruly Englishman pawing the kerbside, and swerved violently. His vehicle swiped the corner of a tray of oysters being carried on the head of an earnest marketeer bent on maximising profits by swift and efficient handling. It was not to be. He crashed into a tier of 'mums,' and shellfish and flowers fell to earth. The florist emerged and beat the fishman about the head with a broken bloom. He retaliated with a shattered oyster-shell. The tanker-driver descended from his cab on high and laid in with invective and a clipboard. An ancient, looking to appease, stooped to pick up petals and shells. Then, doubtless overcome by her sense of impending duty to the departed, filled her black shopping bag with wholesome blooms and a plenitude of oysters, and went on her sorrowful, determined way.

Roundabout ways

A new town bypass has just been built. Whether as a consequence of the specific oyster and chrysanthemum battle I witnessed I know not. In any event, it was true that, before its completion, heavy petrol tankers grinding up to *Andorra*, to off-load fuel for selling to motorists who had crawled up behind them to buy it, passed through the main street; or rather, panted to a standstill in a permanent traffic jam. Hot diesel fumes belched filth and toxicity upon townsfolk and tourists alike. As each holiday season advanced and the air grew hotter and evermore polluted, tourists lingered less and less in the town to do their shopping. The shopkeepers complained that their trade was being ruined, and clamoured for a bypass.

Several small trees were duly cut down, to supply sufficient paper for the *fonctionnaires* to work out 1000 ways of saying 'Maybe,' for a year or two. At long last the imminent approach of yet another August shut-down persuaded someone, his thoughts already dwelling on his family's forthcoming exodus to the *Midi*, to say 'Yes.' Work had hardly begun, before some unthinking *fonctionnaire*, without a care for commerce, opined in public that the streets would soon be rid of tankers; and cars - and tourists. The shopkeepers complained that their trade would be ruined, and clamoured to put a stop to the bypass.

This was a conumdrum such as *fonctionnaires* dream about, in bed, on the beach, and sometimes in the office. It offered the ultimate in logical obfuscation. It was a challenge not just for a few locals, but for battalions of *fonctionnaires* nationwide.

Several small forests were duly cut down, and the paperwork began in earnest. The local newspaper upped its print order. The issue pushed youth unemployment off the back page, and the mayor off the front. Even his photo was consigned to the centrefold.

It fell to an expert in cultivating *les espaces verts* to break the deadlock. Full of capability, though his name was not Brown, he had helped to further the cause of landscape gardening throughout the region. Lifting up his eyes unto the hills, he persuaded wealthy locals to raise their sights beyond their favoured flowering potplants and custom-built barbecues to the horizons that lay beyond. Where all was presently scrub and stone, to him there knocked opportunity. With his devoted team he dug and delved, moved mini-mountains, diverted streamlets, laid underground hoses, planted lawns and trees and flowers until every rich *fonctionnaire* clamoured for a similar private oasis. Not that the proud owners ventured off their terrace when the work was completed, any further than they had done before, but now, as they lay on their *chaises longues,* they could open their eyes and squint at a vista, a *belvédère* that was all their own. And what appealed to them most of all was that people passing by in their cars would slow down and stop, to gaze in admiration.

Profiting from this phenomenon, the Man from the Kew had installed little placards offering his services wherever such cars changed down, through curiosity. He extended this publicity to where they changed down of necessity, at T-junctions and roundabouts.

Then one day, on the road, he had his vision. The road led to the local town, rather than to Damascus, but his vision was nonetheless intense. It too involved conversion: the conversion of every roundabout on the bypass under construction to a landscaped verdant hillock, beckoning the weary motorist to pull off the road and stretch his legs awhile. Thus refreshed, he might feel like wandering into the town square, perhaps even pausing to buy something which caught his eye. What had been attempted elsewhere in Catalonia, could be brought to perfection here in *Riberal.*

The plan was an instant success, not least with the *fonctionnaires*, who had doubtless already thought of it. It has even helped unemployed youth, some of whom, after special training, can now be seen tending the green grass and luxuriant flowering plants on every roundabout. But they are not mere gardening hands. They have learned how to lay underground pipelines and to regulate irrigation. They know what plants to choose for the cold winter, what for the summer. Especially how to select and train plants for display purposes: the Catalan flag vivid with *sang et or*; images of sun and snow; for *Riberal* claims both, situated at *la croisée des passions*; examples of *la fantaisie*; even musical essays in sculptured cactus and floral archetectural forays into Advanced Art. All this, of course, on top of the normal road ganger skills of arranging cones and cambers such that heavy tankers are swayed by centrifugal forces to take the bypass, while lighter cars, pausing in wonderment at the floodlit foliage, - lighting know-how is also a prerequisite - can slew round to a standstill on the road towards town and trade.

As for the *fonctionnaires*, they are delighted, for have they not been able to make good use of their paper stocks by translating their 'original' proposals into appropriate *fonctionnaire* phraseology and despatching them in abundance to other Town Halls in other towns? And the mayor is delighted, too. A photograph of him appeared in the local paper, standing proudly on a roundabout, with youngsters planting flowers at his feet. The photo was on the front page.

It's a dog's life

You are probably wondering by now what the snags are to being six feet up in the Pyrenees, cleaning windows for a living. Sipping wine in the November lunchtime sunshine, I confess I find it difficult to focus on anything dire or deadly except - ah yes - except dogs. To me, French dogs spell disaster, like ducklings, or chrysanthemums.

My study of these quadrupedal curs leads me to conclude that there are only three categories, in my definition: Carried Dogs (*chiens de poche*); Wolves (*guardiens*); and Woofters (anybody's unattended *Titou*). Carried dogs have no legs. They are owned by childless females - that is, those with no children immediately to hand - or whose offspring are allergic to fussy, jangly jewellery, and thus cannot be taken on promenades, like their wet-nosed substitutes, bound to the bosom. Wolves own slender men-about-town, and keep them on a strong chain. Woofters have fringes and fleas and flailing tails. They have no collars and bark all the time because they cannot see, bumping into parked cars while trying to find their owners, small boys or short-sighted, hairy pensioners. They also frequently bump into moving vehicles or window-cleaners on the move, making drivers and cleaners both cry out for a **Law**.

All such beasts foul all surfaces all the time. To me, ever mop-conscious and street-wise, the problem is, let us say, fundamental. To the French, *boulevardiers* every one, the nuisance is merely *en passant*. Ever philosophical, they even say such encounters bring you good luck all day. The only luck I have had is to evade a repetition of the experience for the rest of the day. But that was more likely to be because I was carrying a residual reminder about with me.

Mind you, there are those who find fault with my categories. My good friend George, who is the security officer in charge of safety measures for all branches of a national supermarket chain, and who should thereby be knowledgeable about the perambulatory shortcomings of those who might need at any moment to escape sudden annihilation by fire, assures me that, in his opinion, the derogatory term 'carried' should not be used.

His wife, Brigitte, is owned by such a creature, *Menuda* by name. *Menuda*, which is Catalan for *Titch*, lives in a portable carrier-bag, decorated with embroidered flowers. She wears different costumes and jewels, according to her social engagements: jewels for the town shopping expedition, tartan plaid for the country weekend. She would have no more chance in a supermarket blaze than one of *Riberal's* ninety-year old pensioners, being similarly delicate of constitution and short on leg articulation.

George is adamant that such a refined aristocrat as *Menuda* ought automatically to exact instant sympathy and tender loving care at all times. She should never be termed a 'carried dog', which implies handicap. That would hurt her feelings. With due French tact she should rather be referred to as *'une chienne assistée.'* She is, he would aver, wholly unsuited, because of her well-bred sensitivities, to the four-paws-on-the-ground rigour of life as a 'woofter', or *'chien autonome'*, as George deftly defines such canines, dismissing them with a wave of the hand as *'pas sympa.'*

We had a friend to stay one summer, a cycling addict, who, you will recall, found greeting people the French way difficult while still attached to his vehicle. He found them impossible when a wet nose intruded in the intimate cheek-by-jowl ritual. This friend was an international expert on the mechanics of the body, especially joints and leg action. To him, *Menuda's* legendary immobility was a challenge. One look at her, and he had to be restrained from applying a match to her *haute couture*, as a test. He gave her exploratory jabs with his elbow, when Brigitte was not looking, to satisfy himself that *Menuda's* status as *'chienne assistée'* was no exaggeration.

On one occasion, tragedy was averted by the merest whisker. Brigitte phoned the doggy hairdressing salon, - yes, of course they exist, in France! - for her to be nicely turned out. "Can you offer your service by tomorrow lunchtime?" she asked. "Certainly," a gruff voice replied, " Would you like her turned out as a roast or chops?" She had phoned the cooked meats butcher by mistake.

It behoved us to show shocked sympathy.

A job on the right lines

Here I must make a confession. Such indecent musings led me one day to down bucket and leather before a taxidermist. Now I had thought taxidermy went out with the pressed flowers and antimacassars of the Victorian era. Yet here was an unmistakably 20th century offer to gather up your expiring carried dog, canary or kitten, off cushion, cage-floor or kerbside and return it to you, the owner, if not in full voice, at least as fully filled out as in its erstwhile heyday. You could opt for stranger quarry. Even a prize goat, mountain eagle, or wild boar idly come by could, sooner or later, be reissued: stuffed. Fish, for some arcane, aquatic reason, took longest.

How could such an enterprise prosper, I wondered, in these video-happy days of wildlife in the armchair and animal high jinks on the hearthrug? Overheads, at least, would have to be kept to a minimum.

I needed to look no further than the location of the business. It lurked adjacent to the railway with its fortuitously live electric rail. Painless provision of raw materials at little cost, save bait, seemed a certainty, provided one could wait awhile. And the locals are patient folk, by and large, and used to waiting: for inheritances to be bequeathed, grandchildren to procreate, and pets to wilt and wander and be found dead. Like the Victorians.

I must drop a postcard to my cycling friend.

The mad hatter's tea party

As people got to know me, my social life, even in the midst of window-cleaning, began to expand. People talked about me when I wasn't there, and to me when I was, so that they could talk about me again, afterwards. With my odd accent and odder activity (for a university graduate from the professional classes), I was the talk of the town, to match gossip on oyster quality or green bollards, at least. To start with, it would have been thought impolite to let curiosity loose and accost me. As soon as I was accepted, it became impolite not to.

On one memorable wet afternoon I was invited to tea by *Laughing Man.* I call him this in kindness, since he was in reality a shy, lonely bachelor, of diminished private means. Like me, he was in his mid-fifties, and like me also, destined daily to criss-cross the streets of the little township. But while I did it out of commercial obligation, and proceeded with care, he did it out of obscure psychological compulsion, and (as I have already mentioned), held moving vehicles in risky disdain. He suffered from a nervous complaint which made him chuckle to himself as if at a secret joke. This attracted a degree of derision from a few outlandish tourists. But most locals tolerated his nervous amiablility with typical laid-back wry amusement, and responded patiently to his eager button-holeing, referring to him as *'Monsieur Vache-Qui-Rit.'*. He lived in a little flat in *La Rue de Dix Amoureuses*, a cul-de-sac in more ways than one, and claimed to be from aristocratic stock. He was well educated, and a Royalist to boot. I had thus to be prepared, while wringing out wash-leathers, to engage in commiserations over the outcome of the French Revolution, and even over the execution of our Charles 1st. Although his education was eccentric, he was as likely to catch me out on matters of English history as on the use of elision in French, and roundly castigated my deplorable tendency towards Catalan mispronunciation. It was hard, when concentrating on eliminating *traces* and *taches* to pay attention with sufficient regal deference.

Nevertheless, the afternoon arrived when I found myself sitting down *chez Laughing Man* to a lukewarm brew-up of *thé Lipton*. In our goodly company was also the walking corpse of unruly feet fame. He was, apparently, without the power of speech; which, on reflection, I suppose, was only to be expected. His fellow-guest was a pensioner in pebble glasses and pink combinations. Atop these garish garments he wore a playful grin, like Muttley. *Laughing Man* apologised for the stiff's uncommunicativeness on the grounds that his father was Portugese, but I think the more reasonable excuse was that he had been dead for a week or so. He looked rather pale, propped up against his bowl of even paler tea, which smelt of fish. At least I think it was the tea, though defunct males of Portugese extraction may well retain a whiff of sardines beyond the grave. I believe that is why *Laughing Man* gave us fish forks to butter our cakes with, to put us off the scent, as it were.

I was furnished with magazines featuring the royal heads of Europe, and admonished for burning Joan of Arc. She was an innocent virgin, giggled *Laughing Man*. She would certainly have qualified as equal to the royals, he chortled, were it not for her being a saint already. Muttley, with teeth and glasses a-gleam, swore that he had once been introduced to one of Joan of Arc's direct descendants, a fireman in Montreal. "Rather late in the day," I observed. *Laughing Man* ignored this improper interjection. Discussion swirled and swooped out of control. Muttley's next contribution was how, when he was young, a Canadian father had hit him on the chin for daring to propose to his daughter. *Laughing Man* believes it was because he had never been as handsome as Prince Charles, and therefore couldn't hope to qualify as a potential son-in-law, even among the Canadians.

Any contribution I made to the conversation caused *Laughing Man's* shoulders to shake like Ted Heath's. It's true. I saw him, the next day, two streets away, waving at me, shoulders heaving still with unsuppressible mirth. He spluttered nearer and I discovered the reason for his hilarity: my tea-time defence of Charles II in the story of Nell Gwyn and the monarch's deathbed comment "Don't let poor Nelly starve." I can't imagine why he found it funny, unless it was the name Nelly. But then, I am never quite sure why my French friends find me funny, as an Englishman. They sometimes start to tell me, then collapse in hysteria. Perhaps it's just as well. Like Figaro, they feel driven *"de rire de tout, de peur d'être obligé d'en pleurer."*

Halt! Christmas shopping ahead

As Christmas loomed once more, my insight into my customers' 'back to basics' attitude to festivites was further enriched.

One of their most endearing features, it seems to me, is their religious and political unanimity when it comes to wealth creation As the festive season draws near, and the cash registers and polyester reindeer start jingling their bells, all urban resources are called upon to unite to attract the diffident shopper.

But Christmas Eve itself calls for something special.

The first tactical move is to entice and entrap all moving vehicles in *Riberal*. For this the local authorities employ - simultaneously - three mobile teams, each highly motivated by the thought of overtime payments at such a time, and each highly integrated with the others, although it may not appear so. This is the military secret of the annual Yuletide commercial offensive.

The first team is equipped with brushes and pots of black paint. The second team wields brushes and pots of white paint. These light-armed troops place themselves strategically at each exit from and entrance to the main shopping square, brushes on standby. The moment the church clock strikes midday, and traffic ceases as the holy *heure de repas* imposes its ubiquitous civilian curfew, the black squad starts to obliterate all white exit arrows from the square, while the whites paint in enticing approach arrows at every entry. To ensure vehicular as well as political solidarity, the heavy brigade then arrives with bright red and white brand new 'no exit' signs, which they erect on poles, or string on chains across the exit roads. One street, however, is left wide open. It is pedestrianised. It also happens to be where all the shops are situated: - the *Rue de la Cordonnerie*.

By one o'clock, the first putsch of the traders' campaign, the 'Encirclement of Motorists', is complete. The three squads are dismissed to partake of a pre-Christmas blow-out, a mouth-watering anticipation of oysters.

Next arrives a motorised troop of soldiery camouflaged by thick, protective clothing. Off the back of the truck a swarthy veteran briskly unwinds reel after reel of heavy guage wire, while others off-load a small forest of Christmas trees. A third party, wielding gigantic pliers and wire-cutters, leaps from the truck and begins the 'Ensnarement of Pedestrians' stage of the campaign. Trees are strapped to every lamp-post, every protuberance on every pavement, so that a brisk stroll past the shops is rendered impossible. Anyone not equipped with the self-same wire-cutters, and an axe to boot, will be forced to adopt a slow and wary gait, given ample time for their attention to be drawn irresistibly towards the shining, gleeful window displays.

Over-riding the new civilian roadsigns in a fashion appropriate to military coups worldwide, the truck returns to Local Authority barracks, its occupants to oysters.

By two o'clock, all is in a state of commercial anticipation as puts Advent in the shade. Momentarily, it should be said, for these are Catholics though the State is secular. At such times, this suits everyone admirably.

Soon the square is glutted with cars, overlapping each other like oysters on a plate. To open them and get at the occupants, succulent with cash at this time of year, calls for psychological warfare.

Here is where Catalan subtlety excels. The loud-speakers in the plane trees crackle, prior to booming forth their brain-washing decibels. But not the carols; not the seasonal tidings of goodwill; not the jingle-bells' elbow-jogging exhortation to spend, that a mere Englishman might expect. Oh no. The fairy lights and stars snap on, as usual, but the rhythm is tango, and the song 'Jealousy.' You are instantly transported to sultry southern climes. Those whose experience of rueful Januaries reminds them to watch their wallets by day the moment shepherds begin to watch their flocks by night are bemused as to time, place and season. The mind is unhinged - and the pockets seem to empty themselves unbidden.

As darkness falls, the satisfied shopkeepers wish one another *Bonnes fêtes*. The press-ganged shoppers return laden to their vehicles, beached between trees on every pavement or scuttled on the square. They do not notice that the stop signs and chains have been removed, and they are too weary to concern themselves with contradictory arrows, especially as a kind *gendarme* with a conspiratorial wink is waving them to choose whichever exit-road suits.

Later that night, all evidence of arrows aiding and abetting expenditure will be obliterated, so that good order and discipline might be restored before Midnight Mass. Only the trees and lights will remain during the holiday shutdown. Why? To make sure no-one forgets it is Christmas.

CHAPTER NINE

"Lies yet snow in the mountain?"

"Lies yet snow in the mountain?"

After passing several years here, I find it increasingly difficult to choose a favourite season. It goes without saying, particularly for visitors from Northern climes, that lazy summer days are hard to beat, but that has much to do with leaving behind and returning to grimmer climes. For those of us fortunate enough to live here all the year round, other criteria press their claims. "Choose me," chirps the Spring. I'm unruly and unpredictable, especially in the mountains. You've no idea whether tomorrow I'll be flaunting furs or flowers. It's exciting." "Don't be *blasé* now and pretend you've had enough of my hot languid afternoons, on the beach," drawls half-naked Summer. "You know siestas make sense." "You can't shut your eyes to my colours," says Autumn. "Nor, surely, can your taste-buds ignore the fruit and wine, - and the mushrooms, of course." Winter keeps silent, but beckons the shining mountains to come closer. Whether crystal-clear or misty, Winter in the mountains has a special appeal, a magic touch of intimacy.

Well done....?

It was the end of Autumn up in *Noullogarret.* We were quietly drinking *apéritifs* on the balcony. The street was empty, since the holy *heure de repas* was approaching. The air was warm and the sun was shining out of a blue November sky. For the Catalans, the weather was worth a casual shrug: *"Comme çi, comme ça."* But for us, as the mountains huddled closer in the clear air, it was bliss.

Suddenly, a nearby chimney gushed smoke and flame. The home of a neighbour, the ancient Village Oracle, or Mistress of the Bras, was on fire. We rushed along the street, shouting futile advice, all the more because, in our excitement, we were shouting in English. We trailed a ladder, a damp sheet, a fire extinguisher and a *Fibreglass* fire blanket. The old lady stood in her doorway, handkerchief held to her streaming eyes, shoulders defiantly heaving. "My husband said the kitchen smelled so bad I must have burnt his lunch." Such was her distress, we surmised lunch must be a haunch of wild boar, newly caught by his hunter friends, and much to be prized. "I know he likes his meat *sanglante*, so I tell him I have never burnt his lunch. Never, in forty years of cooking for him. The very idea upsets me. It's not true. I am a good cook, but now the tears fall."

What were we to do? It seemed hardly decent to say: "Quite right, Madame. You are indeed an excellent cook, especially at roasting *sanglier*, as we all well know. It's nothing at all to do with your cooking. It's just that your house is burning down!" But there was no time for words, diplomatic or crass. The heat and flames were threatening to engulf the timber roof-beams.

A neighbour rushed out of his house, eyes popping out of his head with eagerness to help. He was brandishing a bedroom slipper, intending, literally to hop on the roof and attempt to beat out the flames. Another neighbour arrived, put my ladder to the roof, climbed up and wrapped our damp sheet round the chimney-top. For a moment black smoke engulfed us all. We held our breath. Then flames burst forth anew. As a last resort I offered up my very British *Fibreglass* fire blanket. It looked very small and inadequate. The hero on the roof stuffed it right down the chimney. "Useless, utterly useless! It will char and burn too," cried the growing mob of excited onlookers, napkins in hand, furiously wiping their lunchtime lips. "Is everyone in the village eating, do we know? Call the goatherd, mayor, police, helicopter evacuation service, maybe even the fire-brigade!" they variously suggested, grasping at manifold straws.

"But they'll be at lunch also," said another, sagely assessing the situation. "Let us see if the English *truc* thingy-ma-jig is successful. I remember my uncle told me the English put out several fires in London during the war."

I was not certain that *Fibreglass* existed at the time of the Blitz, but I didn't feel it was a good time to pour cold water on anything except the fire. First the flames, then the smoke, gave up the struggle. The sky was once more a welcome blue. We no longer felt able, however, to appreciate the warmth of the November sun's rays.

Mopping their begrimed faces, the villagers withdrew to continue their Sunday lunch. The hero of the hour climbed down from the roof, and returned my fortuitous ladder. "Useful we have British window-cleaner in village," he said. Our neighbour thankfully replaced his slipper, unsinged.

The old lady said: "I **never** burnt his lunch; **never**, in forty years." She turned on her heel and went indoors.

Madonna of the Météo

Every year, at about the beginning of December, we receive a picture postcard from a German friend of ours with the predictable postscript: 'Lies yet snow in the mountain?' The gaudy photo reveals that the sender is basking in the sunshine of some exotic clime - for she is a veteran traveller - where snow is unheard of. When the card arrives we, too, are usually enjoying fine Pyrenean late autumn weather, sitting on the terrace under blue skies, sampling the season's fresh young wine.

Although it is pleasant to hear from friends, I always used to shiver involuntarily, while smiling at the scrambled syntax of the card. There seemed to me to be a fatalistic threat underlying the glum Teutonic humour. It touched directly our vulnerability, for we had never yet experienced a harsh winter in our mountain retreat. Then, one year, it happened.

When the snow came I was ready for it, or so I thought. Not that preparation had been all that easy. When the Village Oracle pointed a quivering finger at red berries on every bush, and shook her fist at a small cloud floating above the distant peaks, muttering the while, I hastily turned on the TV weather forecast for confirmation.

Recently we had been subjected to what the local French TV weather forecaster termed *pluie faible*, which I took to mean rain, but not much of it. She is not, as in the UK, exactly expert in weather ways, rather a media celebrity, with low cleavage, flashing eyes and a nymphet's infectious giggle. I wished, nonethless, that her choice of words had been a little more precise. In fact, we had non-stop rain for three days and nights; and after, frost and ice.

The owner of the electricity generating station, who I think used to act in films as *Fernandel*, claimed we had had 300mm in all, which is something like 12in if my maths is anywhere near accurate. The local stream was a raging torrent, and the mountain road virtually impassable because of falling earth, trees, boulders, landslip, fog and sleet. The owners of the trout farm were cut off by floods and reduced to eating their own trout. The road to the goat farm was also impassable, but fortunately the occupants had a deep-freeze.

I tried to drive downtown one Monday morning to collect supplies, only to find my return route blocked by two enormous boulders, the size of refrigerators. They took me an hour to shift aside sufficiently to squeeze my *Panda* through. Stones and earth were swirling down and past me all the time, so I was glad to get home sodden, but safe and sound.

The same afternoon we found our lower terrace had been swept down by the floods into our neighbour's hen-run. A rumble, a squawk, *c'est tout*: no more pool, no more *poulets*.

Then followed the big freeze. My son and I were returning home on the Thursday evening in the *Panda*, in a very cautious manner, after a hard day's cleaning. My wife was half an hour behind, in her old banger, having stayed in town to do some shopping. Just entering a slow left turn in the road, wide, but with a bad camber, I lost control of all four wheels simultaneously. The *Lady* and I were doing a Torvill and Dean on a lake of black ice, but our routine was unrehearsed. We pirouetted gracefully across the road, waltzed up the steep off-side bank, did a graceful barrel-roll and landed on our roof, back on the road.

There was a hiss of escaping gas. Could it presage explosion, I wondered? No, it was just an aerosol (sweet violets perfume) going off in my son's left ear, while his right received a jet of *Ajax*. The cassette player continued coolly with its carol recital. It was just chanting 'Earth lay hard as iron' when we decided enough was enough, and we had better vacate the vehicle. We crawled out, and I had the presence of mind to turn off the engine - and the music.

Meanwhile a consternation of cars had arrived. People were amazed to hear me muttering about tidying up the chaotic jumble of brooms and brushes.

"Hadn't we better first help the *Lady* cover her *cul* and get back on her feet, for modesty's sake?" someone suggested, pragmatically. They were right, I realised. So we turned her right side up, receiving much help from the goatherd's wife. She believed my insistance in brushing up broken glass and putting the contents of the van to rights was indicative of shock, not of British cool.

The roof-rack and ladders protected much of the roof - and both of us - from receiving a dent or two. If we had had skis on top maybe we would have had no damage whatsoever. (The *Panda* boasted *Val d'Isère connections*, after all!)

All was not well with her chassis, however, and the *Lady* was declared decrepit, destined for instant retirement. At least we escaped without a scratch. My son believes our salvation lay in my determination to continue steering when halfway up to Heaven. He claims that such was my skill when airborne, doubtless benefitting from my training as an RAF pilot, I was able to make a controlled approach to *terra firma*, which, although I was in inverted flight mode, precluded stalling and nose-diving into the tarmac, engine first. I take much comfort from this filial gesture, the more so because my son did eventually injure himself as a consequence of independent *panache*. He fell on his backside while demonstrating to on-lookers how slippery the ice was. With the *Lady's fesses* so recently waving inelegantly in the air, I had felt they didn't really need further proof. A notice might have helped, however, for when the sanding wagon came up the very next day, following my telephone call for action, the driver, much to his embarrassment, turned it on its side in the self-same spot.

By the time I had acquired a replacement vehicle, a *Fiesta*, it was time to think of snow chains. High time!

Once more I tuned in to the forecast. "Continuing fine," preened the Madonna of the *Météo*. With a fine disregard for such professionalism, I drove down to *Riberal* to equip myself. The garage boasted an out-of-season sunblind sale, with free choice of a *pin's*. Not an encouraging start. "The sort of snow-chains you need you will find in *Perpignan*," was the unconcerned comment, so off I went, somewhat ruefully, some forty-five kilometres to make the prudent purchase. Back in the village, no-one was impressed. "You need winter contact tyres," they chorused. Down I went again to town, this time avoiding all garages that were challenging pessimists to buy sunblinds.

The tyres were purchased, mounted, and the bill paid Only then did the proprietor take me aside and say: "I hope you don't mind my impertinence, but I happened to notice your snow-chains. With your new high-contact tyres they will bind on the chassis if you turn sharp corners. But then," he reflected, trying to cheer me up with gallic logic, "perhaps you live up a fairly straight road." I pointed out that the mountain road was all sharp corners. "Ah, pity," he pondered. Then: "As it happens, and as a great favour, because we don't normally stock them, I can swap your chains for a pair which will fit." I noticed his were slightly rusty, though mine were brand new. But now was no time for bargaining. I had no wish to go all the way to *Perpignan* again, so I accepted with alacrity. I went home in triumph, hoping it would snow soon, and give me a chance to test my acquisitions.

It did. Five winter's worth in one dumping. We were cut off.

Moribund mounds, a metre deep, blocked the road, and drifts turned my car and adjacent wood-pile into identical giant dollops of whipped cream. "One day they will send the snow-plough," neighbours said, reassuringly. "Last time it took two weeks." I made a hasty check of storecupboard and deep-freeze, and forbade a visiting female friend of the family to feed the Head of the Nature Reserve's cat on our tinned tuna. She resorted to smoked salmon. The neighbour, cut off in a distant mountain village, where his Nature Reserve Conference was getting closer to Nature than intended, telephoned her to ask after the creature. Emboldened by her response, he ventured to request she also feed his rabbits, chickens and horses. I quickly calculated that acquiescence might at least mean rabbit pie and chicken casserole. If we were cut off for five weeks I might even go native and try horsemeat. I told her to say "Yes."

My wife phoned a day or so later to say she was holed up in *Toulouse*, making up for missing me by attending a film festival by night and day. I expressed my sympathy with delicate forcefulness.

Three days later the snow-plough arrived. The primaeval drama of battling with the elements had gone to the driver's head. Atop his massive machine he charged into the village, thrusting bergs, boulders and bushes before him. He savaged my wood-pile, an 007 ripping off its white coverlet as if expecting to find a scantily-clad SMERSH agent cowering thereunder. He descended on my new car, a Sweeney Todd wielding a giant blade. Slathers of snow flew like shaving-soap in all directions, and instantly my reversing mirror dangled down like a sliced-off ear. He riccocheted past the other vehicles huddled forlorn in the car-park, leaving them a naked flock of badly shorn sheep.

The next day I drove downtown. Mini-avalanches continually shed rolling boulders, sharp stones, earth, ice and small trees upon the narrow road and upon those rash enough to be in transit. To linger was to risk a damaged roof - or worse. To proceed at any speed above a writhing slither meant a puncture or unintended vertical descent via the treacherous snow-girt verge. I opted for the puncture.

I slewed into the side of the road where the slope was minimal but the snow, in consequence, 'deep and crisp and' - cold as charity (without the charity). I consulted my newly-acquired handbook. Instructions on jacking up the vehicle were plentiful and illustrations vivid. Unfortunately, they referred to every type of *Fiesta* but mine. When my *marque* was mentioned, explanation was scant and obscure. To compensate, prohibitions were emphatic and the dire conseqences of error spelt out in multiple exclamation marks. By a process of elimination I concluded the only place to insert the jack lay right under the vehicle, where the snow lay deepest. I took the jack and the spare wheel out of the boot, but found there was no wheel spanner. A brisk half-hour walk to the next village, whence I might telephone home for help, was just the thing to restore circulation, I told myself, fiercely.

When my son duly arrived in my wife's car with the spanner, we set to with a will. Five minutes would see the job done, we thought. But we had under-estimated the forethought of our garageman, who, mindful of the increasing number of car thefts, had skillfully hidden the anti-theft key for the fourth wheel nut where even we could not find it.

Down to the garage in the other car at the aforesaid slow slither, quick consultation with the garageman on the psychology of hiding places and the profitability of the tyre business in wintertime, a vehicular slither up again, and the job was done. Should you possess such a vehicle, know that it only takes two hours to change a wheel.

Such sagas deserve a postscript. I should have anticipated, being in Catalan country, that one would be forthcoming. On arrival for the second time at the garage, the owner looked ruefully at the damaged tyre. "I think you will need a new one," he said, "but I have no more winter tyres in stock. I'll order you one. Delivery will only take three weeks, and in the meantime I can put the original summer tyres back on. Of course, you realise that with those tyres your snowchains won't fit. I can't change them back for the ones you gave me, as I've just sold them. You'll need a new set. We don't normally stock them, as you know. For the sort you now need, *"Vous les trouverez à Perpignan."*

Round robin in the snow

As the snow retreated, it left devastation in its wake. The road was strewn nightly with falling debris as the mountainside alternately thawed and froze with each twenty-four hour cycle. In two places the road itself began to subside, and one of the villagers got up a petition to get the local *fonctionnaires* to do something before we became isolated by total subsidence. He had quite a time at first getting signatures, but then the idea, as it were, snowballed and all the villagers rushed to sign. *Flying Lobster's* cousin wanted to attach a list of personal complaints going back to 1937, and was quite difficult to restrain. The *Fernandel* look-alike who runs the electricity station and has frequently to go downtown, not only signed but broke into into the Village Oracle's (Mistress of the Bras.) home dragging her forth, even though she is illiterate, to make her mark. Her husband said it was all a big fuss, and he didn't mind being cut off anyway, provided his wife had enough *gigots de sanglier* (wild boar haunches) in stock, to roast - giving her an old-fashioned look - the way he liked it: *sanglants.*

"It's all very well for you lazy selfish retired people," yelled the electricity king, temper on a short fuse, "Some of us, like *Monsieur Huit-heures* here, have to go down to work each day, to pay for your pensions. You must sign!" The only villager not to sign was our very own village idiot, whom we called the TCB. Not catching his real name on first acquaintance, but merely noting his relationship to the Oracle's hunter husband, we referred to him, of necessity, as the Toothless Catalan Brother-in-law, or TCB for short. His role was that of handy *Man-about-Village*, and very useful, too, as he was always ready to lend a hand, and always there when you needed him, since he couldn't drive and never went down town or ventured at all beyond the confines of the village. He smiled memorable encouragement, however, his single tooth gleaming like one of the icicles hanging overhead.

In the next village our friend got everyone to sign except the mayor, who had turned away the snowplough, saying there were not enough residents overwintering in the village to warrant the cost of clearing it. Our friend was furious, having the problem of shovelling a pathway through snow a metre deep half a mile or so to his hungry cattle. He decided to construct his own snowplough and attach it to the front of his tractor. He forthwith cleared his pathway, the square and pathways to those elderly villagers who were still in residence. He then gleefully piled all the cleared snow up against the mayor's garage door. His partner *en concubinage* decided that, if the *fonctionnaires* didn't do something quickly, she would boycott the school bus on grounds of the children's safety. Catalan villagers are determined folk, quite used to moving mountains - or getting them moved, if the need arises.

Our own mayor, too, had a difficult time with his cattle. He went searching at dawn for a baby calf, marooned up in the mountains, found it in a snowdrift still alive, and brought it safely down on his shoulders. It weighed forty kilos (about 90lb) and he spent nine hours in sub-zero temperatures, frequently falling over in huge drifts, or sliding uncontrollably down the icy escarpment. Half an hour later, he was sitting at the mayoral desk, beneath an elegant photo of President Mitterand, totally unperturbed, bruised and bloody and covered in cowmuck, catching up on the formal paperwork of his office. It was thus he gladly signed the petition, which took on a slightly rural smell. "That should make it all the more authentic!" he said, smiling hugely.

Surface tension

In Catalonia, it is not just the intimacy of Winter which attracts, but the way it springs surprises on you. By night, the temperature may drop well below zero, as freezing fog drifts up the valley. By day, snow flurries may make you hurry home to a welcome blaze of logs in the hearth. Yet a day later, the wilful Northern wind, the *Tramontane*, may blow the sky quite clear of cloud in a matter of minutes, letting the sun burst through enough to tempt you in no time at all to take *apéritifs* in shirt-sleeves on the balcony. The impetuous South has taken over. It is not the change, but the suddeness of it which astounds and delights.

So it is with the character of the locals. We were having a fire-side winter tea, English-style, with friends whose families originally came from Spain. They had acquired, to all intents and purposes, the laid-back manners of the French: a quizzical, philosophical approach to life's ups and downs; a calm acceptance in general that *'c'est la vie'* - 'that's life.' Little vestige, as they munched their scones, of Mediterranean passion.

It happened that on that same afternoon their nubile fourteen - year old daughter had gone riding high up in the mountains with a handsome French divorcee whose innumerable female conquests were the talk of the village.

Time passed. It got dark and snow began to fall gently. Our concern gave way to growing anxiety. The horses were not all that easy to handle. What if one had slipped on the ice and thrown its rider, who might even now be limping down the long and winding track, hours away from home? What if the fall had been more serious: concussion, perhaps, one rider having to stay beside the other till rescue should arrive? We must collect blankets, a thermos of hot tea, perhaps brandy, bandages, and all the paraphernalia of first aid. We must telephone the mayor to say what we intended, and go off up the mountain in the van to look for the missing couple. Not wishing to add to the parental anxiety, we said little as we hustled on our winter coats, but had little doubt they shared our views and practical policy in every particular, all the more because we knew they were both trained mountain rescue personnel.

We stopped at the parental home, to make, as I thought, the aforesaid appropriate provisions. Imagine our astonishment when the father appeared, suddenly utterly Spanish. He stood aggressively in the doorway, carrying a hunting rifle. Nothing else. *"Montez!"* - "Get in!" he said. There was no arguing. We bumped up the mountain track in silence, apart from the throbbing of the diesel and the whining of the two pet dogs, who knew something was amiss.

Finally, we could go no further. Ice was causing the van to skid dangerously towards the precipice at every corner, and the falling snow cut visibility to a few yards. My wife was feeling car-sick and our friend's wife was nursing a huge bruise on her spine, caused by her slipping on the ice when we dismounted to see if we could distinguish any tracks in the deepening snow.

The journey down was even quieter than the ascent.

Suddenly, in the beam of our headlights, we saw them. The two riders, safely astride their mounts, were descending slowly but directly through the forest to avoid the ice of the track.

Everything that followed was blessed anti-climax. Father could do nothing but drive carefully down the adjacent track, keeping the riders in sight. By the time we had reached the village, all of half-an-hour later, his killer fury had evaporated quite, and given way to sentimental Spanish gratitude at finding all was well. Gradually the rifle became an embarrassment. No mention was made of it at the moment of reconciliation. The explanation was that one of the horses had escaped, when the couple had dismounted at the top, and had taken a hour to be found and recaptured. This excuse was accepted almost cheerfully, with sunny Southern nonchalance. The handsome young man was invited in for a beer. We went home.

But the daughter, when she heard next day what her father had been prepared to do to defend her honour, was in seventh heaven.

A Hamlet without the Prince

As December advanced, it became clear to us that, unlike Bing Crosby, we had no need to dream. Christmas, this year, would be white. But that was where our traditions finished, and Catalan ones began.

On Christmas Eve, we went to a *Pessèbre* - a 'Living *Crèche'* performance in a lovely old 18th century church in a neighbouring mountain village. The ambience was quite mediaeval, for all the Catalans wore their regional, rather than biblical, costumes and offered appropriate regional produce, including oysters and *muscat* in *porros*, at the crib. These were removed at a quiet moment in the proceedings, to be preserved for the subsequent midnight feast.

The *crèche* was certainly 'living,' with a real baby in the crib and a goat threatening to vault the altar rails. The baby was removed, just before the adoration of the shepherds, for an unscripted nappy change, so they had to worship an empty cradle, which seemed rather sad. The congregation, however, was sentimental and practical in equal measure. They prefered poignancy to pungency.

The costumes and local touches made the ceremony simple, but moving. Not so the music. It was, I fear, a talent contest, with every vocalist believing himself or herself to be holding centre stage at *La Scala* at the most dramatic moment of personal passion. Even when the melody the soprano was singing was a charming Catalan lullaby, it sounded like Brunhilde in the *Metro* suffering from Doppler effect as the organ got more and more distant in time and tonality.

The best vocalist was, truth to tell, the goat. He began quietly enough, happily munching the Christmas greenery within reach, delicately avoiding electric flex and fairy lights, musing contentedly the while. When décor was depleted, he tried the iron altar rails, but they were not to his taste at all. He then set up a forceful, but not overstated complaint at not being allowed to cross centre stage to the greenery and Christmas tree on the other side. It was, by comparison, a modest expression of feeling, I thought: contemplative, and entirely in keeping with the occasion.

A lamb called Gunedilde

The following morning the Catalan implications of the Season of Goodwill were brought home to us on our very doorstep.

I should explain that, by this time, my wife had succumbed sufficiently to village ambience to become obsessed with sheep. I should have noticed the signs, but as it was Christmas it seemed appropriate to shed a tender tear for the animals round the crib - even in tribute to the vocal goat. In fact our village had no crib, as the church was closed, but there was a stable, or rather a *bergerie*, right next door. We could smell it through the wall, full of warm and woolly snufflings and shufflings, quite close enough to give the Christmas Story more than the usual sentimental credence.

No single star shone that night. Instead, the mountains shepherded a whole flock down the Milky Way into our valley, to watch and wait. On Christmas morning, there was a new-born lamb on the straw.

There the story should have ended. Not for the saintly mother *brebis*, but for us mere mortals. It was not to be. Replete with the dinner of the small hours: unexpected oysters, unbidden *boudins blancs* (white sausages), *risqué Roquefort* cheese, not to mention the clichés of turkey and wine, I failed to recognise the signs. The Catalans have a way of celebrating Christmas that rather takes your mind off it. The old shepherd observed my wife's expression, dived into the *bergerie* and emerged carrying the bleating lamb over his shoulders. He placed the snow-white woolly bundle in her arms and said "Here you are. Her mother's rejected her; and the other sheep are going down to their winter quarters tomorrow. She's all yours to bottle-feed *au biberon. Bon Noël!"*

It is best to draw a veil over the lamb's secular upbringing. It's true my wife gave her the royal name of *Gunedilde*, a Flemish princess who became the First Lady of Catalonia, wife of *Count Wifred le Velu* (Wifred the Hairy). The general woolliness seemed appropriate, though I doubt whether the royal personage washed her curls in *Woolite*, as befell our *'Gunny'*, one warm Spring day. Suffice to say that by the summer she had become a fine figure of a *brebis,* and my wife was thinking pullovers. My thoughts were on mutton chops.

CHAPTER TEN

Workers' playtime

A ll work and no play makes Jack a dull boy," they say. And, I might add, without time off, Jack makes a dull window. With summer visitors stumbling over my bucket, their small children applying sticky fingers to every square metre of glass in *Riberal*, except where notices protected it, I decided it was time for me, too, to take a break.

Blood-brothers

A sedate and befitting pastime, I decided, might be to join an outing of fellow workers. A few weeks before, one of my customers had remarked: "You look young and in good shape." "It's the window-cleaning keeps me fit," I had replied, flattered, and unaware of what was to follow. "In that case, you can give blood. What's more, all our donors from *Riberal* are going with their friends and supporters on a jaunt to Spain. You can come too, if you'll proffer a bare arm when called upon." Thus it was that I found myself heading for Spain at six-thirty in the morning, my ears deafened by rousing *risqué* Catalan songs, which lurched into Spanish as we neared the border. The trip included a visit to the ancient Greek city and wine jar depot of *Ampurias*, appropriately chosen to give us a thirst for lunch.

En route we left our bus to mount a curious 'train' - three ramshackle wagons towed by a tractor decked out as a railway engine, complete with bell and cow-catcher, to wind us through the narrow streets of a historic village, which the coach could not negotiate.

The first shock, reverberating through the village square, was the change of music. "We welcome aboard two English," said our leader. Suddenly the Sunday quiet of the village square was rent by the music of the band of the Grenadier Guards, playing, as a tribute to our presence, *'Blaze Away,' fortissimo*. The train moved sedately, at a snail's pace, between the silenced buildings and shocked terraces. Villagers clutched tightly their second Sunday glass of *muscat*. A woofter barked. That was all. Nobody seemed to mind. The dog stopped barking. Then we climbed, fearfully, precipitously, out of the village. An unaccostomed but essential third glass of *muscat* was poured, shakily, behind closed doors.

The train twitched sexily in and out the tourist-titivating ramparts. It flaunted *joie de vivre*. The music played on. To our astonishment, we found ourselves teaching our fellow passengers '*The Lambeth Walk,*' complete with ear-splitting 'Hoy!' On rubber wheels we trod where angels fear to, encroaching even on the hallowed *heure de repas*. This was not because our own gastronomic needs had been overlooked, but because the Spanish dine some three hours later than the French. Since we were not yet in Spain, we had, perforce, still to go hungry, whilst our compatriots fed. Indeed, when we finally arrived at our appointed hostelry, some suggested that the blood in our veins was already running a little thin, and, in the light of our forthcoming professional obligations, hoped fervently everything would soon be done to put things right.

It was. We ate well. Although the meal itself was satisfying beyond measure, second helpings descended on us like manna, until our gratitude itself became bloated. *Charcuterie paysanne, poisson en croute, boeuf bourgignon, sauce forestière, fromages variés, crème Catalane,* accompanied by a profusion of red, white and *rosé* wines, capped by a vintage sparkling dessert white, *méthode champagnoise,* and all at a *prix compris* suited to those on a pension. I was glad Catalan cuisine flourished on both sides of the border.

In the afternoon we paused upon a windy knoll where birds of prey were esconced, viewing us askance, awaiting their daily liberation. We stooped, crouched, cringed in readiness. Each bird of prey was loosed individually in strict rotation, in recognition of its presumed undisputed ownership of the windswept territory we were momentarily usurping. Each in turn swept down to scoff the paltry offering from our outstretched, nervously gloved, hands; then off, up, aloft again, into the wind and the weather. Cameras clicked inconclusively, without ever a capture. A desultory plane heaved itself up and across the sky and whined disconsolately northward, like a dog with its tail between its legs. Merlins, falcons, eagles without a care, reclaimed their unruly kingdom.

But for every king, the clowns. Such were the vultures. They flew like princes, but on the ground hopped and hobbled like crippled fools. "Do not be alarmed," said our guide, "they will not try to eat you ; they are only interested in carrion, that is to say, meat that is quite dead!"

Nevertheless, they all took an unnerving interest in one old lady in our party. Perhaps they knew she had once been a blood donor. They hovered knowingly over her head, then landed nearby with a bump. They started to peck with exploratory eager intent at her shoes and handbag. True, she had not joined in the *Lambeth Walk*, nor indulged in second helpings over lunch. More tellingly, since her arrival on the exposed hillock, she had remained somewhat immobile. However, we deemed her still alive, and felt a twinge of sympathy for her aggrieved vocal remonstrance with the vultures: "Not yet, not yet, you beasts!"

Before reboarding the coach we gave full-blooded commitment to buying up the nearby market. Brazenly we rattled towards the Customs post, then still operative, banking on the strength of our good deeds. We were flagged down, somewhat nervously. "But **we** are the blood-donors of *Riberal!*" our leader cried, our coach a-clatter with its tell-tale load of pottery, olives, sherry and brandy, all duty-free. We burst into a sentimental patriotic Catalan drinking song, and the Customs men fell silent. The useful thing to bear in mind is that all Catalan songs (even lullabies) are sentimental, patriotic, and have to do with the abundant riches of the sunny homeland: - that is, wine, with the odd peach thrown in. Because the songs are so generously all-embracing, you don't need many of them. In consequence, everybody knows all of them, and can launch into a convincing chorus, suitable for all purposes, on all occasions.

The customs men waved us through, enthusiastically. Some even started to sing along.

The next day we had to give blood. I feared the alcohol content might not be conducive to restoring a healthy mind in a healthy body, but I was told that the important thing was to be joining in celebrating the bi-centenary of the Rights of Man, bloodshed and all, in a practical way.

I was astonished to learn, a few days later, that we had each earned a reward for giving blood: free anti-tetanus injections. A question of take and give.

Altogether now!

By now the house and garden were fit to be seen, the business was flourishing, and the holiday period was over. I decided I had time to take up a hobby. In England my recreation had been choral singing and direction, so, emboldened by a pressing invitation from one of my favourite customers, I joined an amateur group which had gathered together to sing a few folk songs to raise funds for charity.

We found ourselves under the tutelage of a certain Dominique, a *nonne civile,* or lay nun, who had initiated the idea. She was a stocky, wholesome lady with a neatly laid-out four-square face, framed flatly on either side by featureless ears which billowed gently whenever melody beckoned. Her life-long passion for music-making was expressed solely through her eyes, crossed, it would seem, in permanent schizophrenic bliss.

She arrived with two large keys to open the School of Music, where we were to rehearse, but failed to position them correctly in the locks, which were arranged vertically in the door. People were reluctant to offer help, in case she were offended. At last a beefy Catalan, of an independent cast of mind, who said he had only come to sing *soliste*, put his shoulder to the door. It creaked and split a little, and we were in.

Once inside, Dominique decided to hold a voice test. The women, some two dozen of them, could only manage five notes of the scale. It took half an hour to get through them painfully, one by one. All were deemed contralto or mezzo - not a soprano to be found except for an English friend of mine, who had been a professional singer. She sang three octaves and won a round of applause. The men, as vocally unendowed as the majority of the women, numbered only five, including the self-appointed *soliste*. I managed to sing two octaves, and was also embarrassed to receive a round of applause, judiciously rather less prolonged.

Dominique turned for encouragement to her portable wheeze-box organ. It offered a variety of starting notes to choose from, provided she pumped hand bellows vigorously the while. Most people chose notes to suit themselves, and began to sing the 'air' when they felt ready. The conductor waved at them in a faintly encouraging way, from time to time, to indicate staunch acceptance of the inevitable, and waited for the 'air' to peter out, which it did as people got out of breath, or wanted to chat. To make matters worse the 'air' was in Catalan, which the French strongly objected to, as they couldn't understand the words.

My problem was slightly more *recherché*. I realised the four-part setting we were attempting was, in reality, set for two tenor parts and two bass, not for the usual four parts: soprano, alto, tenor and bass. Dominique did not recognise such trivialities, and proceeded to involve everybody. The sound was monstrous, with an octave gap between squawkers and growlers. The only vocalist to rise above it all was the self-appointed *soliste*, who insisted on singing the tune regardless, and not his part, "because I know it and have come to sing!" He was too independent to oppose. And we all acknowledged that, without his beefy expertise, we would still have been shut outside, waiting to begin the rehearsal.

We turned in desperation to something in French and *très simple*, which the conductor had dreamed up, hand written and photocopied. The 'music' read thus:

```
              la                la
Tenor: 1 la      la 1 la / 1 la      la 1 la / 1 la 1 la 1 la / 1 la 1.la 1 la /
           la
      1 la      la 1 la / ha              /          rallentir
      Je t'aime, 1 je t'aime à jamais (2 temps à vide) sans crainte
      - / 1 sans crainte / infiniment / BF / BF / BF
```

Well, how did you get on? In case you are feeling as puzzled as I was, BF means *bouche fermée*, (with mouth closed), nothing ruder. With voices trembling and hands shaking we responded to the impossible instruction to sing it straight off. It was not deemed a success.

When Dominique realised that our sightreading left much to be desired, she decided to forsake the wheeze-box organ and turned to the piano. Rashly selecting yet another song, she started to play over the alto and tenor parts together, but did so with crossed hands. My first thought was that ocular deficiency or simple superstition had finally overwhelmed this good soul. I looked again: the left hand was playing the alto line, while the right hand picked out the tenor part, **two** octaves lower than written. Slowly there dawned on me the divine logic in her approach. Since the tenor part was indeed written in the treble clef, a devout personage such as she might assume it should duly be performed by the right hand. A mere single octave lower would create cacophonous collision with the alto line. Thus her triumphant resolution of the problem. Never was the music of the spheres more adroitly kept in orbit. But never did fallible mortals of tenor persuasion attempt to sing so low.

Gaining confidence, Dominique turned her attention to the musicianship (or lack of it) of our ensemble. As was fitting, we humbly submitted our ramshackle musical ensemble to her bifurcate vision of perfection. At last we were singing as one, while she conducted as two.

Her concentration was fixed in all directions, simultaneously. Looking at the basses - or so they believed - she upbraided the tenors, although all thought the altos were supposed to be singing at the time. We were primed for action as never before. "Imagine the Good Lord has kindly placed meathooks through your ears, to raise you up so you can more joyously sing His praises!" she told us. We instantly stood upright as a regiment, though the *soliste* thoughtfully fingered his ear. "Open the lung, depress the diaphragm!," she admonished. "Imagine instead you are breathing the good clean air of the countryside!" The Principal of the School of Music, who had just arrived, and in whose room we were assembled, looked a little piqued and quietly opened a window.

There remained the little problem over pronouncing Catalan words correctly. A frail elderly alto proffered a phonetic rendition, warmly received. Dominique thanked her. *"Alors, avec la musique, je vous démontre!"* she beamed, doubly. It was true her interpretation clearly owed little to French, which was a relief. But then neither did it ressemble what we could recall of the Catalan example. Suddenly the penny dropped. True to her calling, Dominique was joyously intoning the verse in Latin.

They decided, after heated debate, to call the choir *'Ar y Sem'* which in Catalan means 'Now and Forever.' I had a feeling they could forget the *'y Sem''* bit. The choir would never survive a second rehearsal.

Sorry, Beethoven

Steadying itself after this experience, the choral executive decided to ask me to take over direction of the choir. My arm action when wielding my *mouilleur* in pursuit of my trade had clearly been noted.

Christmastime came round again. For children, and for their long-suffering parents, that meant concert-time. That was why, as conductor and, as such, ex-officio member of staff at the School of Music, I found myself shivering back-stage in the unheated wings of the local cinema-cum-theatre, about to lead my singers on the stage.

In the spotlight, a frowning twelve-year old was biting her lip trying to persuade the piano to obey her so that tiny pianist and huge instrument could appear to be proceeding sedately. But the concert grand, like a big black unruly woofer, would have none of it. Beethoven between its teeth, it galloped away *prestissimo*, heading for home and the *Mecca* of the last bar, the girl's fingers chasing pell-mell after it, throwing caution and accuracy to the winds.

Behind me my little choir were anxiously following the chase, noisily shuffling their feet, their positions, and their carol sheets. They knew their turn was next. I began to wonder whether this untried flock, in spite of earnest intent, would prove more undisciplined than the black dog. I flexed my conductor's arm, and twitched my baton, in readiness. Suddenly I was tapped on the shoulder by the Principal. "Oh Mr. *Weentaire*, I am asking are you willing to sing *Beethoven's Ninth Symphony* in a floating nightclub on the Med. in two weeks? I must know as soon as you come from the *scène*."

Instantly my imminent modest carol repertoire forsook me. Stonger, fantastic images surged and swayed before me. *Beethoven's Ninth*? **My** little choir? And all at sea in a nightclub? "I'll have to think about it," I muttered. "Yes, but let me know tonight. And now she is finish. I shall present you; come along on the *scène*." "My name is not *Weentaire*," was all I had time to murmur, before the Principal announced: "I present Mr *Weentaire* - ah, no, I mistake, Mr *White-ear*, who is preparing *Noël* for us tonight."

Somehow we sang. Somehow the flock didn't panic. And somehow we trotted by the reassuring pallisade of the penultimate barline together.

But once in the Green Sheep-pen, there was no respite. We had to decide about Beethoven. Flushed with its immediate success, the choir was unanimous. "Of course we must accept. Beside, there are twelve dishes, each prepared by an individual chef from each of the twelve members of the EEC, to celebrate the arrival of the Year of European Unity. And you must be there to eat the English dish. No-one else will." Thus the matter of *Beethoven's Ninth* was settled on the principle of gastronomic *entente cordiale*.

Later that evening, as a true patriot, I accepted the challenge and was handed my sheets of information. The most important related, not to Beethoven, but to food. It was a press hand-out headed *'Dégustation des Douze'*, roughly translating as 'A Taste-in by the Twelve.' It waxed lyrical over Greek mushrooms and Portugese scallops; ravioli ravishingly stuffed with secret meats from Italy. Even the dish prepared from Dutch cheese was made to sound exciting through the virtuosity of the French language in glorifying all things gastronomic. Tactfully, in order to keep the juices flowing, no mention was made of the British entry, or, rather *entrée*.

The second item was the invitation proper, in full colour, on card, entitled *'L'Europe Gastronomique,'* with the participation of the Association of Cafés, Hotels and Restaurants and the *Amancier Rociero* Artistic Group from the city's Spanish Centre, with full address supplied, to meet instant public response. There followed secondary acknowledgement of support from the University Orchestra and Choir and String Ensemble of our Principal, with whom, I supposed, we were to be anonymously associated. The printing was superimposed on a pale grey image of a passably sea-worthy vessel, clearly sailing in mid-Med. Overleaf, however, though this time in full colour, the ship appeared to be in some difficulty. Against a backcloth of a night without stars, she seemed to be irredeemably beset by fire from stem to stern. A lurid distress flare lit the smoky heavens, and you were enjoined, in neon sky-writing, to set your evenings aflame - and, self-evidently, yourself - by going aboard to participate in a discothèque ominously entitled 'La Machinerie', which I took to mean 'The Works.' Subsequently, if you needed to offset personal fire damage, for a sou you could become a millionaire in the glittering casino adjacent.

The third offering was, indeed, the music for *Beethoven's Choral Symphony*, or, rather, music for the choral part. I have to admit, for modesty's sake, that even this had been curiously modified to fit on one side of a photo-copied single sheet, two verses only of the *Ode to Joy* remaining. Clearly, our music-making was to be curtailed by the love of food, and no way were we to be allowed to 'play on', to give 'excess of it' or otherwise. Moreover, tenor and bass parts had been prudently amalgamated. This was just as well, as I only had one tenor, a gentleman, whose claim to fame was expertise on the musical saw, and whose singular self-confidence was matched by unprecedented unreliability. The choice of key was equally undemanding, unlikely to provoke indigestion in choir or audience. Consequently, it bore no relation to the high-flying original. One risky element remained: the words were still in German.

A rehearsal duly took place in the *Conservatoire* at *Perpignan*. Vocal representitives of the Twelve arrived by coach from the University. Their pulsating vehicle slewed imperiously into the carpark, forcing our breathless little minibuis to take evasive action, and lurch to rest on a scenic lawn.

I was optimistic that the adroit editorial trimming, cutting Beethoven down to after-dinner, *digestif* proportions, so to speak, would mean a short rehearsal. I should have known better. No self-respecting Frenchman can tangle convincingly with the Teutonic tongue, especially when the words have to be not only spoken, but sung. We tussled gamely with *umlauts* and gutterals for two hours. Someone suggested omitting verse two and singing verse one twice instead. This, French pride would not allow. Finally, a bespectacled German student was brought to the fore, marshalling a hand-held mike, to coach us in the mysteries of bristling end-consonants, usually airily dismissed by speakers of Latin-based languages. The mike muffled them sufficiently to be acceptable to French ears and reproducible by the French larynx, and we were allowed home. After twenty-three repetitions.

Came the great day. Arrived in the seaside resort, we made our way self-consciously along the path leading to the shore, to the amazement of a single local taking his woofer out for an evening fouling. All, that is, save the *Maestro* of the *Scie Musicale*. Always the individualist, he clambered over *Fibreglass* rocks and broken floodlights, whose bare electrified leads gleamed in the moonlight and hissed at him as he lumbered past. Trudging through the dog-muck, we eventually reached the quay, all dutifully clad in modest black and white. All, that is, save the *Maestro*. He sported a flamboyant multi-patterned pullover and cream slacks. Even his shoes were different. They were still clean.

Before us glittered the boat. The name **'Le Lydia,'** finally convinced me that the French are not, nor ever have been, a truly nautical nation. I was not surprised, therefore, to find that she was firmly embedded in concrete. Clearly, the disco-dancing and dining were not to be outbid, in the interests of verisimilitude, by the rhythmical contortions of a bout of *mal-de-mer.*

Once on board, we proffered our invitations and were hustled below by two *matelot*-bouncers. "Just time for a little rehearsal," beamed our Euroconductor, assuming the intimidating role of musical bo'sun, and stowing us discreetly aft, among up-ended emergency settees and stand-by ship's catering tackle. After an hour or so, we were thankful to be interrupted by the disc-jockey, ranked Captain, who suggested we get on parade to see if there were enough room for us on the disco dance-floor, or whether some of us would have to be thrown overboard. We were herded amidships, where the disco tune-up was deafening, dazzled by rotating searchlights and mirrors, presumably signalling *Mayday.* A hundred and twenty weak, we were crammed together as on a slave ship, hardly able to breathe, let alone sing. Even though we were obliged to hold the music an inch in front of our noses, in the fluctuating shadows the words were impossible to read. Using a ship-to-shore loud hailer, our conductor decided we had better resume rehearsal elsewhere, until the disco tempest abated. I noticed the hold was dressed overall in the flgs of the Twelve. Ominously, the Union Jack not only lacked the Scots Saltaire, but was flown upside-down. Distress notwithstanding, it was evident the purloined message spelt out the French expectation that each of us this night would do his duty.

An hour or so later, the disco began in earnest, with an ear-splitting acknowledgement of British pop. We were then entreated to join in the latest 'Rap.' I did my best with a mixture of prudently untwisted Twist, befitting both my age and my epoch; a modest adaptation of the Sailor's Hornpipe, in honour of **'Le** Lydia,' and my usual watered-down Scots *fandango*, in tribute to the missing Saltaire. Something was still missing, however. Although hot and bothered, we were not yet aflame, as the invitation promised. It took the Spanish *troupe* to set us alight, with a fiery display of *Flamenco*. I should have known. Every event in Catalonia sooner or later strips off its superficial French cool for its underlying Spanish fire. Everyone joined in and only the desperate call *"à table!"* on the loud-hailer put the French firmly back in charge of the musical mutineers.

The dishes of the Eleven lived up to their reputations, and the British down to its. It was supposed to be 'toad-in-the-hole', but I suspect the chef had been led astray by his dallying in French cuisine, à *jambes de grenouille*. I dared not speculate further. Let me just say there was no detectable trace of sausage. Soon, however, British food and French *ferveur* were both forgiven as the wine passed round and and the music and dancing began again.

A final rehearsal and kit inspection were commanded, then on we trouped. Singers were still tucking in wayward garments and trying to uncrumple wine-stained shreds of *Beethoven's Ninth* by smoothing them out on the bare shoulders of the girl in front. One student, who had assumed the lotus position wearing shoes, to indicate he was the only singer fit to take the lead in a forthcoming performance of *Léhar's 'Land of Smiles,'* set in China, could not be unfolded in time. He was carried, like a Buddha, into the finale shoulder-high. The *Maestro à Scie Musicale* entered bent double, using his copy to scrape a breaker of curling cream off his trousers. He had failed to find his sea-legs, even after several glasses of wine, and had fallen athwart a billowing French dessert which truly went over the top. "It was a good job I wore my cream trousers after all," he muttered brightly, from under someone's skirt.

"For the *Finale*, the only way we can get attention after so much happy racketing, will be to sing the *'Ode to Joy'* quietly and, er, I suppose, rather sadly," concluded our bemused bo'sun. "Sorry, Beethoven."

And so we did. But, since nobody wanted a down-beat ending to the celebrations, ours wasn't the *Grand Finale* after all. An improvising group from Guadeloupe, adorned with beautiful sexy lead singer, upstaged us with a pulsating, hand-clapping rendition of *'Oh Happy Day!'* I'm not sure Guadeloupe qualifies exactly as European, but then, neither the French Constitution nor world geography is a strongpoint of mine In any case, it turned out the group's *ad hoc* conductor was English.

Postscript

It is now five years since I began my great Adventure, and time for me to retire once more. I have been fortunate to find a replacement to carry forward the little enterprise with like enthusiasm and an eye for things of interest. For what I confess I had not bargained for when I began is the bonus of golden experiences that my upfront exposure to the workaday Catalan way of life has brought me.

What can I offer in return, when I now go down to *Riberal* as a *retraité*, without my leathers and ladder? Just a hundred handshakes and smiles, that's all. But it's enough.

Thank you customers and citizens all for offering me the privilege of sharing in the *douceur de vie* of French Catalonia, not as a mere onlooker, but as a fellow-worker cleaning windows in your midst: a *Riberal* artisan in all but name. *Tout est bien qui finit bien.*